THE AMERICAN BILLBOARD 100 YEARS

THE AMERICAN BILLBOARD 100 YEARS

BY JAMES FRASER

HARRY N. ABRAMS, INC., PUBLISHERS, NEW YORK

CONTENTS

ACKNOWLEDGMENTS
7

PREFACE
8

THE EARLY YEARS
10

THE BILLBOARD GOES TO WAR
24

THE GOLDEN AGE OF BILLBOARDS:
THE TWENTIES
44

THE BRIGHTER SIDE OF
THE DEPRESSION: THE THIRTIES
68

THE 1940S: BACK TO WAR
84

NEW CONTENT, NEW STRUCTURES, OLD CHALLENGES
96

THE CREATIVE ENERGY OF THE SIXTIES
122

CREATIVITY, CONSERVATION, AND CONSCIENCE
148

EPILOGUE
186

BIBLIOGRAPHICAL NOTE
189

INDEX
190

CREDITS
192

EDITOR:
SHARON AVRUTICK

DESIGNER:
RAYMOND P. HOOPER

Library of Congress Cataloging-in-Publication Data

Fraser, James Howard, 1934–
The American billboard : 100 years / by James Fraser.
p. cm.
Includes index.
ISBN 0–8109–3116–8
1. Billboards—United States—History. I. Title.
HF5843.F73 1991
659.13'42—dc20 91–8450
CIP

Copyright © 1991 Outdoor Advertising Association of America, Inc.
Published in 1991 by Harry N. Abrams, Incorporated, New York

A Times Mirror Company

Printed and bound in the United States of America

◆
ACKNOWLEDGMENTS

Without the continuing help of Joe Blackstock (Patrick Media), Robert Collins (Gannett Outdoor), Doug Watts (Watts and Company), and Roland McElroy (Outdoor Advertising Association of America), this book could not have been completed in so few weeks. (These individuals are not, however, responsible for error or oversight.) Lynn Steck provided useful criticism as well as picture editing services. Sharon AvRutick, the book's editor, and Ray Hooper, the designer, took the trials as challenges.

Others who have assisted in various ways: Michael Adams, Jack Banning, Carla Binder, Eleanor Cohan, Emma Dana, George Dembo, Nancy Fletcher, Caitlin Fraser, Sibylle Fraser, William Herzog, Mark Horan, Susan Jacobs, Silvio Lam, Greta Loebl, Robyn Lystrop, William Mannheimer, Robert and Jean Reed, Leonard S. Rubenstein, Leslie Schreyer, James Shuptrine, George Theofiles, and René Weber.

Four individuals who merit recognition for historic reasons are Marvin Goldstein, painter and professor of art history at Fairleigh Dickinson, who, in 1972, suggested that the university begin an outdoor advertising archive; the late Odell Hathaway, an industry leader who donated the first major collection of material; Frank Cawl, then-president of the OAAA, who carried the project association-wide and provided funds to build the reference collection; and Budd Buzek, then-president of the Traffic Audit Bureau (New York City), who first promoted a history of the industry in 1978, and who added extensively to the archive's holdings and inspired further collection efforts.

The Naegele Outdoor Advertising Company of Minneapolis kindly placed a substantial number of 35mm slides at our disposal and was on call for various queries and advice. Gannett Outdoor Advertising's Fairfield, New Jersey, plant also made its archives and reference collection available. Other companies provided varying degrees of information from their files.

PREFACE

The bold, framed, and freestanding billboard is an American invention.* Its scale fits the American landscape and conveys its advertising message directly, without the distractions intrinsic to newspapers, magazines, radio, and television.

The billboard's size and style of presentation, as we have known it throughout most of this century, have been directed mainly to automobile, bus, and train passengers. Its smaller urban counterpart, affixed to the sides of buildings or integrated into the walls of bus shelters, often contains the same images for the same products but adjusted in scale to fit the pedestrian viewer. But regardless of its size, the billboard of our concern is intended to do one thing—sell.

The following illustrated account celebrates this medium in America by calling attention to those entrepreneurs, artists, and companies that developed its potential. What you will find is neither a history of the American poster nor even a detailed account of what we will call outdoor advertising from colonial times to the present. That must be left to others. What you will find is a brief historical sketch of but the last 100 years of the American life of this medium, which had its prototype in the Egyptian upright slabs of stone termed stelae by the Greeks, announcing decrees, warnings, and laws in public places.

★Although billposting as an occupation and the leasing of space on which to place posters in Britain predate the American experience by a decade (1861 vs. 1872), British concern for a standardized, freestanding billboard structure did not develop until the early twentieth century. In the United States, by contrast, regulated structures of several manufactured styles were already in use in the 1890s.

The bill poster—shown here at work in 1891—was not at all a universally popular figure in his day. The author of the 1896 publication *Street Types of Great American Cities* wrote, "The bill poster is an unmitigated nuisance, and his existence ought to be forgiven him only for the occasional delight he furnishes the children."

THE EARLY YEARS

When setting out to find the origins of today's relatively sophisticated multisheet billboards or the dramatic, painted bulletins with cutouts on Sunset Strip in Los Angeles, one would hope for more than Jared Bell's garish 9 x 6' posters for the 1835 circus season or his *Anaconda Serpent of Java*, produced in the same year for the Zoological Association, a touring show.

Nevertheless, the large outdoor poster (more than fifty square feet) seems to have had its origins in New York in Bell's printing office, which had recently installed a newly modified Napier cylinder press manufactured by Richard Hoe, also of New York. This improved press, which could accommodate larger sheets than earlier models, was to give way by 1846 to another Hoe-manufactured press able to accommodate an even larger sheet. This opened the way for an industry that could put a message and picture on a series of paper sheets which, when assembled, were limited in size only by the constraints of the structure to which they ultimately needed to be fastened.

The circus and the theater of mid-nineteenth-century America were natural clients for this method of advertising. The circus had been using large posters, almost as large as those Bell produced, since the early 1830s. Throughout the century, newspaper offices were the primary production centers for such posters, and this work, because of its seasonal character, could be integrated into the more regular flow of the publishing schedule. Gradually, color lithography became the preferred method for poster production and by the late 1870s the color woodcut posters of the early circus and theater days were becoming a thing of the past, although some poster printers did continue using the woodcut process.

P. T. Barnum, the best-known mid-nineteenth-century circus and entertainment figure, was but one of numerous personalities in the circus industry at that time. Printing for the circus and the theater and the attendant supply industry formed the basis of what was eventually to become the outdoor advertising industry. Although most posters in Barnum's day customarily measured 126 x 84" (made up of three sheets of 42 x 28"), many poster users, including Barnum, thought in larger terms. The manner in which these early large-scale advertisers had their posters mounted (or where) would make latter-day poster company executives cringe. Photographs of even turn-of-the-century circus posting give some indication of the sights that greeted pedestrians and travelers in nineteenth-century America.

Anyone wandering along the roadways on the outskirts of larger American towns and cities at that time was regularly assaulted by a clutter of crude signs and fading and fluttering paper on board fences and other surfaces, to say nothing of painted rocks of all sizes, from boulders to rather substantial cliff displays. Few surfaces were sacred; the itinerant billposters, as well as those who were usually in the employ of the circus or local theater, did not hesitate to paste posters on any available surface—including other posters they may have hung a few days previously.

Towns and cities were just as cluttered as the landscape surrounding them, so much so that by the close of the Civil War, community activists had checked some of the greater abuses through local legislation. By this time, the major users of outdoor posters saw the advantages in self-regulation and marketing that organization would provide.

The first move toward association of poster advertisers in the United States took place on August 27, 1872, when the International Bill Posters' Association of North America was formed in St. Louis. Advertisers had already begun leasing space on sides of buildings and public wooden fences as early as 1867. This was the same year in which the firm Bradbury and Houghteling of New York initiated a nationwide painting and posting service for adver-

This typical chromolithographic circus poster was produced for Barnum by the renowned Strobridge & Company in Cincinnati sometime around 1870, judging from its low serial number. Strobridge & Company, founded in 1867, was a leader in circus-poster printing and became one of the major printers for the billboard industry as it developed.

tising outdoors, just in time for the opening of New York City's elevated railway in that same year.

The "El" was a major advertising event, not just a transportation wonder. Almost overnight, a forest of pillars was created, it seemed, for the partially regulated as well as the unregulated sectors of the expanding outdoor advertising industry. The thousands of risers on the hundreds of stairways leading to the train platforms multiplied the number of available surfaces at eye level throughout the city. Although their size limited advertisers mainly to product names and short phrases, this challenge to succinctness was good schooling for the beginning industry's creative people.

Responsible posting services began to appear in the 1870s and 1880s. Thomas Cusack (Chicago), established in 1875, and O. J. Gude (Brooklyn), in 1878, joined the firm of John Donnelley (Boston), founded much earlier, in 1850. (These names are remembered to this day, and the Donnelley legacy continues in a number of forms.) Still, unaffiliated one- and two-man posting services proliferated and multiplied the clutter of weathering paper throughout the settled part of the country. This directly stimulated the need for further controls through additional organizational efforts. The first state outdoor advertising association was formed in Michigan in 1875 with regulatory, marketing, and fraternal concerns. Other states were to follow.

By 1890, the members of the International Bill Posters' Association, the affiliated state associations, and a growing number of manufacturers were ready for a strengthened national association. On July 15, 1891, these interested groups met in Chicago and formed the Associated Bill Posters' Association of the United States and Canada. The purposes: to promote a greater understanding of the poster medium, to provide an expanded nationwide organization for coordinating the services offered by member companies, and to continue to address the ethical concerns of early industry leaders such as the founding president, Edward A. Stahlbrodt of Rochester. It was a small group of farsighted men who were keenly aware of the industrial potential of the country and the possibilities that the poster in some future standardized form could have as an advertising medium for manufacturers.

The planning and preparation for the 1893 World's Columbian Exposition in Chicago was no small stimulus to these men who saw the hitherto-unparalleled creative energy sparked by the planning as a portent of national and world industrial leadership. Though they were going to be important participants, these sixteen men gathered at Chicago's Great Northern Hotel had little notion of how rapidly their industry would expand in the next decades. Four of them, Stahlbrodt, Frank A. Fitzgerald (Milwaukee), Al Bryan (Cleveland), and George Leonard (Grand Rapids), were the prominent founding members. All remained major forces in the industry and the association into the next century.

Shortly after the founding meeting, the association's executive board arranged for Cincinnati lithographer William H. Donaldson to redirect the emphasis of one of his existing periodicals, *Billboard* (which in time became the music industry's main trade journal), and make it the official journal of the Bill Posters' Association. This arrangement continued for several years until discontent over Donaldson's practice of using the journal to serve the interests of nonmember companies provoked the establishment of an independent journal.

The Bill Poster, A Monthly Journal Devoted to Outdoor Advertising first appeared from the Chicago office of the association on February 22, 1896. Robert C. Campbell, a former principal of the Forepaugh Circus, and in 1896 the new president of the association, was named editor. Although not appearing on the masthead of the new journal, William W. Denslow (who later gained fame as the illustrator of L. Frank Baum's children's classic, *The Wonderful Wizard of Oz*, published in 1900) created the design for the cover and titling throughout and continued as the journal's illustrator for the first year of publication.

The importance of a well-edited industry journal and news organ was widely understood by poster leaders, and the contribution of *The Bill Poster* through its several name changes over the next four decades confirmed their vision. From its outset to the time of its suspension in 1931, the publication was unrelenting in its editorial mission to provide articles on the aesthetics and history of the poster along with news of the political, economic, and technical concerns of the outdoor advertising industry.

The first editor gave considerable insight into the industry's life in the closing years of the century when he recounted in the January 1906 issue of the journal (at that point called *Billposter and*

Right: A cover by William W. Denslow for the monthly journal of the Associated Bill Posters' Association, founded in 1891. Denslow also illustrated L. Frank Baum's 1900 children's classic, *The Wonderful Wizard of Oz*.

Far right: It was said to cost only four and a half cents a day to maintain this 1900 eight-sheet poster for Pillsbury's flour (8'10" x 6'9") in the greater New York area.

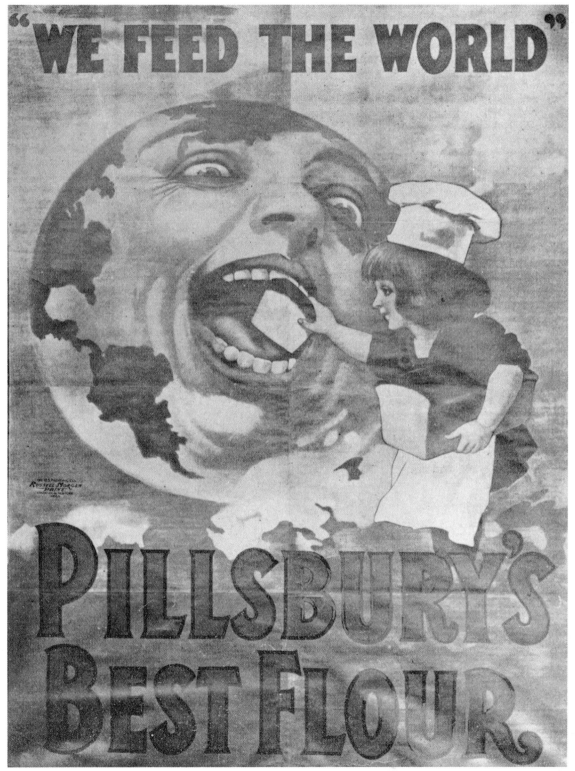

Distributor) something of those turbulent years: "With the birth of our official journal, every member began to think he had a right to play politics, so that when in July 1896 Al Bryan became the chief executive officer he was...kept busy pouring oil on the troubled political waters and tried his utmost to eliminate all factional feelings and cement more solidly the members of the Association. When in July 1897, James F. O'Mealia came in as president, ...he found all kinds of trouble brewing between the 'ins' and the 'outs,' the employing billposter and solicitor, and the troublesome question of the New York situation." (The industry was approaching open conflict in New York City with the rivalry between the New York Billposting Company and the A. Van Beuren Company. The former, not an association member, wished to join, but only one company per city was allowed—and in New York it was Van Beuren. James O'Mealia was ultimately able to resolve the situation with a territorial agreement.)

A complicating factor in this local dispute—indeed a problem of the outdoor advertising industry nationwide—was the question of where to place the posters. Then, finally, in 1900, a standardized structure was created to hold posters of three, eight, and even sixteen sheets (each measuring 42 x 28"). A major step toward standardization—long sought after—had been taken.

The concept of placing a poster on a structure especially designed for it, rather than simply pasting it on a fence or the side of a building, had been the goal of industry leaders since 1871. This single development, while seemingly modest, was necessary in the effort to make the billboard a medium with an identifiable framework. The standardized structure allowed the advertisement to be placed in the landscape or cityscape with a certain authority as a medium; this authority was not lost on existing—as well as potential—clients. Yet, unanimity of purpose did not characterize the Associated Bill Posters' Association. At the 1902 convention in Milwaukee, members divided into two factions: those who were committed to this simple but far-reaching step and those who weren't. The corporate names in the first group hint at their prescience: National Biscuit, Armour, Coca-Cola, Kuppenheimer.

Standardization and self-regulation were closely related and perceived by most association members as the means by which the outdoor advertising industry could gain general acceptance. Anti-billboard campaigns were a regular source of industry concern. Even before World War I they were national in scope. The American Civic Association, concerned about improving urban life in general, initiated a campaign against all outdoor signage as well as the organized outdoor advertising industry. These concerns were elaborated upon in a widely distributed booklet, *The Billboard Nuisance* (1908). Since 1904, *The Ladies' Home Journal* had featured a regular monthly column by J. H. McFarland that called attention to particularly shabby billboards or outdoor signs and published retouched photos of how the same site might appear if the billboard were taken down and the site improved with plantings, a lawn, or a meadow. This monthly effort may have reached as many as 4,000,000 readers, extrapolating from the *Journal*'s circulation of over 1,000,000 in 1903. Such a direct campaign was undoubtedly a factor in pressuring the industry to deal with its delinquent association members.

But more significantly, it focused on those nonmembers who neglected their on-premise signage or nonstandard billboards. This latter group and its excesses invariably brought out the anti-billboard groups, which tended to lump all signs, billboards, and indiscriminate poster placement together as being of one industry, one culprit. In many cases, there was little the outdoor industry could do except appeal to the sign owners as good citizens to improve their sites. Sometimes, these requests worked.

The industry, however, was usually more successful in disciplining its own, who increasingly saw the value of maintaining an attitude of community concern and responsibility for the maintenance of both site and structure. Incompatibility of poster artwork with community standards was less an issue. Vulgarity and the double entendre were simply absent from the billboards of that era, much as they were in magazine and newspaper advertising, although the feminine ideal of the period was frequently called upon to promote this or that product.

The general appearance or design of the billboard or large-scale poster of that pre–World War I era was seemingly a culture removed from the then-new American poster art of the single-sheet size. These smaller, sophisticated images began appearing in the 1890s to advertise theatrical and musical performances, books, periodicals, bicycles, and the services of printers and lithographers.

This twenty-four-sheet Spanish-American War recruitment poster (c. 1900) was one of several major productions sponsored by the members of the Associated Bill Posters' Association.

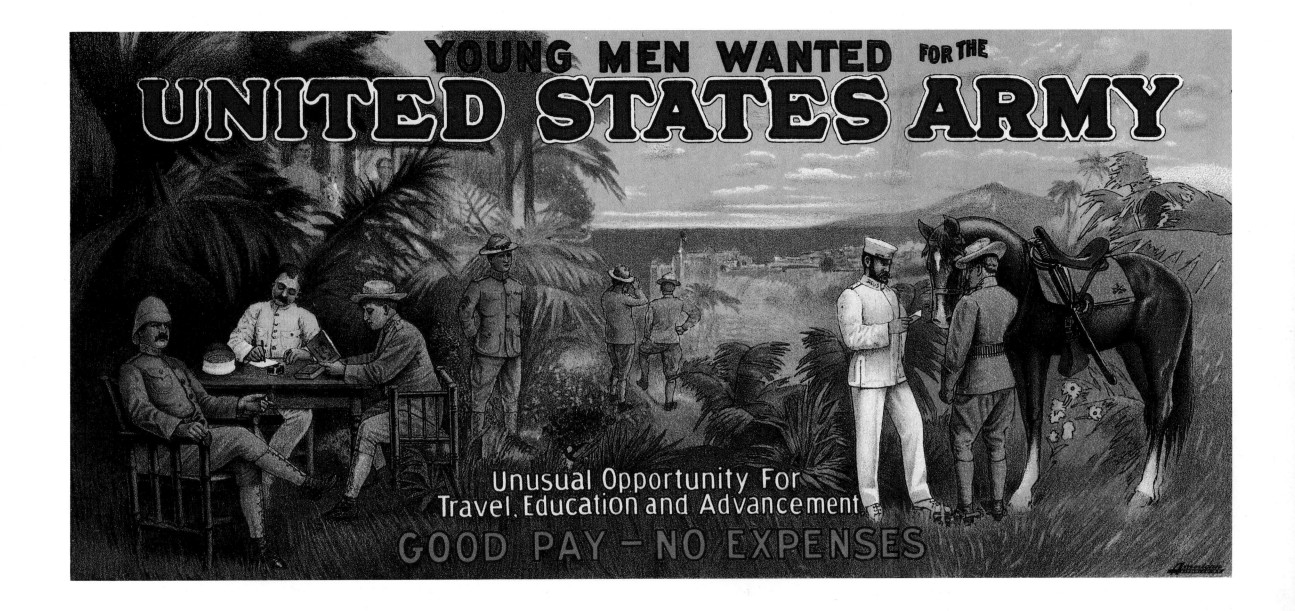

The Quaker Oats man was first used as a trademark for a small Ohio milling firm in 1877. Not until 1890, when the American Cereal Company took over the smaller company, did the Quaker Oats trademark become widely known. By 1891, the man's face was on the company's cardboard containers throughout the country.

Right: John Green of Durham, North Carolina, is credited with the first use of a bull on small sacks of tobacco immediately after the Civil War. This sixteen-sheet poster from around 1908 is just one of many designs with which this product was marketed.

Overleaf, left: A week before Theodore Roosevelt returned from his African expedition on June 18, 1910, this twenty-four-sheet billboard (lithographed in six colors) appeared in most major American cities.

Overleaf, right: Foster and Kleiser bill posters with their wagon in Seattle, 1910. Poster companies also employed men to follow the advance man as he went from client to client selling the designs. The men in the truck would be ready with paint to bring to life whatever arrangement was agreed upon.

It would perhaps be unfair to hang large-scale billboards of the era side by side with the single-sheet work of such major poster artists as Edward Penfield, Will H. Bradley, Ethel Reed, Louis Rhead, or Maxfield Parrish. Many of the outdoor plant owners and industry leaders recognized the difference in the quality of design between the billboard and these small advertising posters.

The pages of *The Bill Poster* called attention to the work of these Americans along with the renowned poster makers of the era, Frenchmen Jules Cheret and Henri de Toulouse-Lautrec and the Swiss Eugene Grasset. The majority of billboard clients, however, were content with the inartistic style of the staff artists working for the lithographic plants that served the outdoor industry.

In the second decade of this century, several important industry decisions were reached. In 1910, the association established a licensing arrangement for official salesmen or solicitors giving the association better control over their actions and thus protecting the advertiser from "unfair and discriminatory treatment in the placing and execution of his bill posting orders."

In that same year, the association rated poster printing plants and firmly enforced plant operating standards (Class A—excellent service, recommended; Class B—good service, meets association requirements; and Class C—does not meet association requirements). These ratings appeared in the national directory of members before the name of the city or town, thus indicating the quality of service available there.

These several steps to improve the industry had an immediate effect. Within eighteen months of the implementation of the classification system, the 3,000 plants in the association had filed reports indicating the condition of every poster panel in the country. Current and potential advertisers were encouraged to examine these reports. In this same time period, members collectively spent more than $1 million in upgrading their plants and replacing the wooden surfaces of varying age with the new steel billboard frames that had been increasingly in use in these years.

In 1912, the association changed its name to the Poster Advertising Association, Inc., in keeping with the conscious effort toward breaking with the negative connotation of "billposter."

The next year, continuing concern about the public image of the outdoor advertising industry provoked the association to es-

tablish an education committee to serve a public relations role. Public service posters were viewed as a responsibility of the industry, and its practice of filling "open boards" with messages ranging from the inspirational to safety concerns has continued to this day. During periods of war, the industry has responded by taking upon itself a shared responsibility for mobilization. In peacetime, the concern has been for those causes that could generally improve society.

A marketing refinement came into being in 1915 with the creation of the National Outdoor Advertising Bureau. Its purpose was to conduct the outdoor advertising portion of business advertising agencies had with their various clients and to regularly inspect the "showings" in the field. The bureau remained a substantial force in the industry until its dissolution in the mid-1970s.

In 1916, the outdoor advertising industry volunteered for military service.

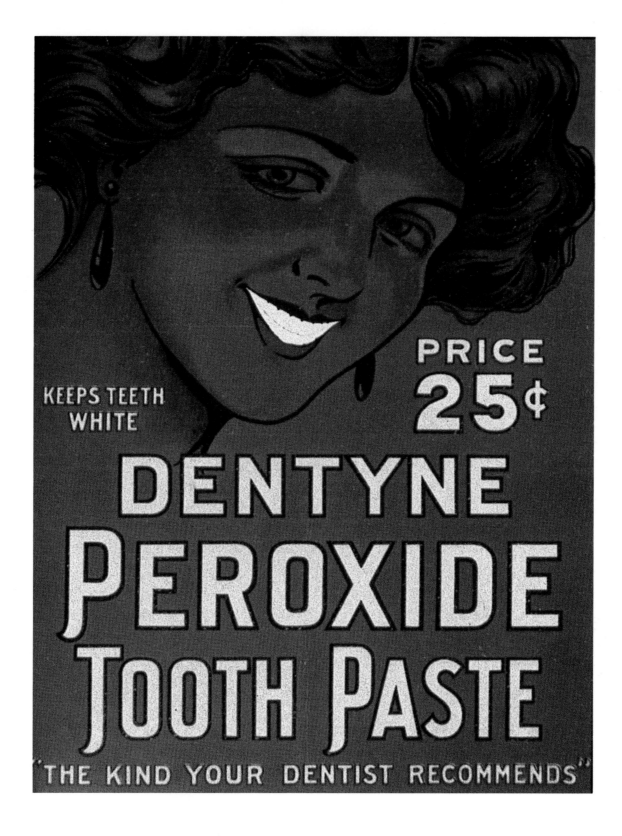

Left: The Uneeda Biscuit boy in his yellow raincoat and hat first appeared as a Nabisco trademark in 1898 in full-page color advertisements in national magazines. By 1911, when this sixteen-sheet billboard (8'10" x 13'3") appeared, Nabisco had already been using outdoor advertising for several years.

Although Dentyne Tooth Paste's first appearance on the market is not known, Colgate was selling toothpaste in jars in 1896 and in tubes by 1906. This eight-sheet poster appeared around 1911.

The Munsingwear label was first carried on gentlemen's underwear in 1886. The Martin Johnson Company, which owned Munsingwear, released this poster promoting children's underwear in the spring of 1911.

Right: George Hendee began manufacturing Indian motorcycles in Springfield, Massachusetts, in 1900. By 1915, he was ready to begin the largest billboard campaign of any motorcycle company up to that time with this twenty-four-sheet poster.

THE BILLBOARD GOES TO WAR

Through its depiction of a multinational group of seamen, Henry Reuterdahl's 1917 Navy recruitment poster (31½ x 43") emphasizes the need for allied nations to pull together in wartime. By the time he produced this poster, Reuterdahl had spent more than a decade with the U.S. Navy as an artist-correspondent.

Overleaf: This vivid film poster says it all about what the silent screen had to offer movie audiences of 1915. It was created by International Art Service of New York City for the Universal Moving Picture Company.

"Huns Kill Women and Children!"
It was staring him in the face,
Telling the tale in headlines
Of the deeds of a hellborn race;
Telling of dastards' doings,
Black murder hurled down from the skies
On nursing babes and mothers—
Such a slaughter as Germans prize....

"Huns Kill Women and Children!"
They are doing it now, today.
Murdering Red Cross nurses,
Dropping bombs on children at play.
Get in the fight to stop them;
In France men are showing you how;
Join the Marines! Go to it!
And the time to enlist is NOW!

From "The Appeal of a Poster"
by N. A. Jennings,
reprinted in *The Poster*, September 1918

Should we have to fight the war without the inspiration and cheer of posters, songs and verses, it will be a reproach to our education and our form of society. Russia at her worst never lacked song; France has both songs and posters; British poets and artists have done their share to help their country. It is an ill day if futurism and cubism in art have put the country in a state where no one seeks or can produce anything better than the posters of last spring.

From "Wanted: A Vital War Poster,"
an editorial statement in *The Poster*, October 1917

On the evening of April 7, 1916, a group of artists, cartoonists, illustrators, poster industry leaders, and others met for dinner at the Hotel Astor in New York City. The purpose of the meeting, called by Herbert S. Houston, president of the Associated Advertising Clubs of the World, and Barney Link, of the Poster Advertising Association, was to stir the art, design, and advertising communities to help mobilize industry. A poster maquette of a somewhat-less-than-convincing Venus de Milo dressed as Columbia with the superscription "Armless" served as a backdrop for the speakers.

Howard E. Coffin, chairman of the program, urged that the best insurance against war was national industrial preparedness. He was followed by Barney Link, who spoke for the outdoor advertising industry. With a confidence peculiar to industrial leaders of that era, he urged: "If you distinguished artists will give us the product of your varied talents, the poster men of America will display it from New York to San Francisco stating the case for industrial preparedness. If you will give us now a store of war posters calling the nation to arms we will, on the possible outbreak of war, put them on 50,000 poster boards in this country in twenty-four hours, shipping allowed for."

Of the artists listening to Link's impassioned plea, only Louis Fancher had any significant experience as a poster artist. No one would claim that he was a major poster maker of his time, but if Fancher had created nothing other than his twenty-four-sheet theater poster *Sumurun* (1912), he would be deserving of a place in American poster history. He did go on to make a few war posters of distinction, one for the war film division of the Signal Corps, *U.S. Official War Pictures* (1917), and one for ground support of the U.S. Army Air Service. However, he is perhaps best known for his *Collier's* covers in the early part of the war, a series that also included

LAUGHS

TEARS

BEAUTY

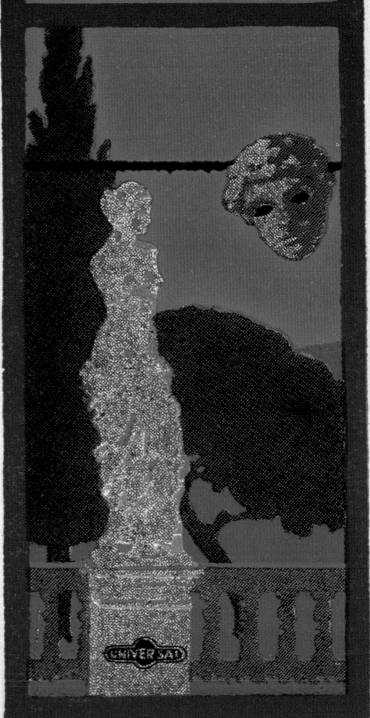

PURITY

THRILLS

SURPRISE

the work of such better-remembered poster makers as Edward Penfield, Herbert Paus, and Adolph Treidler.

The name of James Montgomery Flagg, who also attended this meeting and created the Columbia backdrop, surely needs no introduction today, but at that point he was an illustrator new to the poster field. Within a year, though, he made his reputation with the era's best-known recruitment posters: *First Call* and *I Want You for U.S. Army*. These images, both produced in 1917, were extraordinarily effective, even if they did lack a certain originality. Flagg's "pointing Uncle Sam" has gone on to do various kinds of duty in imitated and parodied form here and abroad up to the present. (A widely remembered example from recent decades is Steve Horn's turning the concept around for the Help Unsell the War organization, an anti-Vietnam War client. In this use in 1971, a bandaged Uncle Sam declares: "I want out.")

Of the other artists gathered for this first meeting, only Henry Reuterdahl created a poster of any lasting interest with his *All Together* (1917), an appeal for unity among the naval allies. G. R. McCauley contributed a somewhat controversial poster maquette for the first Liberty Loan, in which he depicted a stern, pointing Statue of Liberty commanding: "You Buy a Liberty Bond Lest I Perish" (spring 1917). Adolph Treidler, so the story goes, was asked by C. D. Gibson and DeSales Casey a few weeks later to create a softer approach than McCauley's, and over a weekend he produced his *Have You Bought Your Bond?* It is generally accepted on Treidler's testimony that his poster was printed first, and it was thus the first government-sponsored poster produced after the United States entered the war. Treidler went on to create a number of memorable posters for various war effort campaigns while carrying out a few commercial and cultural commissions at the same time. His 1916 poster for the Newark, New Jersey, 250th anniversary celebration won him considerable attention, which brought increasing numbers of commercial and cultural event commissions over the next twenty-five years.

Though war was still at a distance at the time of this first meeting, when it was finally declared, on April 6, 1917, the poster industry was prepared. Wake Up America Day, a government-inspired attempt to mobilize all sectors of the population, was declared for April 19. Two posters by James Montgomery Flagg announced the day, one with a sleeping Columbia and the other also with a woman, but of indeterminate costume reference. The first was the more widely distributed, not only in the forty-eight states but in Hawaii, Alaska, and the other U.S. territories as well.

In April 1916, a second and equally important meeting of poster artists, painters, and Poster Advertising Association officials was convened at the Navy Publicity Bureau's New York office. Discussion centered on how poster and billboard advertising could be adapted for the U.S. Navy's needs on a nationwide scale. Poster artists attending or otherwise agreeing to participate included Francis X. Leyendecker, Charles B. Falls, Herbert Paus, Tony Sarg, Howard Chandler Christy, James Montgomery Flagg, and Charles Dana Gibson. All agreed to serve without pay. A few of the painters who were contacted and who likewise agreed to serve without remuneration were N. C. Wyeth, George Breck, George McManus, James Daugherty, Willy Pogany, Mahonri Young, and George Bellows.

The news of such prominent illustrators and painters volunteering quickly spread through the art schools in the major cities. The students at the Art Institute of Chicago responded by sending this telegram to the chairman of the Society of Illustrators in New York in late April 1916:

Greetings! At a mass meeting of the students of the Art Institute of Chicago, April 16, the following resolution was adopted:

"Resolved, That if art is of value to the nation at any time, it must be in an hour like the present.

"That the 25,000 art students in the United States constitute an army trained and equipped to render its country a kind of service to be given by no other body.

"That posters and cartoons are urgently needed to bring before the people of the United States again and again such truths as are contained in the President's appeal to all the people of the nation, urging them to join the great service army.

"That every art student in the country should at once address himself to participation in this work."

Are you with us?

With the keynote phrase "Made from Palm and Olive Oils," the Palmolive Company emphasized the cleaning and skin-care properties of Palmolive soap. The girl in the design was taken from a large painting by Clarence Underwood.

A gathering of Charles Dana Gibson's committee of poster artists, illustrators, and painters in New York City sometime in 1917. From left to right: Jack Sheridan (advertising designer, *Collier's*); Wallace Morgan (illustrator); Wayman Adams (president, Sculpture Society); unidentified; Charles Dana Gibson (president, Society of Illustrators and chairman of World War I poster committee); F. DeSales Casey (art director, *Collier's*); Frank Sheridan, standing (artist); Adolph Treidler (poster maker and illustrator); Harry Townsend (illustrator); and Charles Buckles Falls (artist).

Right: In 1917, if you needed a spare "shoe"—as tires were then called—the Fisk Rubber Company wanted to make sure it would be one of theirs. This twenty-four-sheet poster by Maxfield Parrish launched Fisk's Art in Posters campaign.

The Art Institute will hold an exhibition of National Service posters. The ten standing first in quality will be a gift to the government. Further information following.

Charles Dana Gibson, president of the Society of Illustrators, responded positively and the movement gained momentum. Businessmen unrelated to the outdoor industry came forward to offer prizes of $500, $300, and $200 for the best-designed posters—sizable amounts for that time.

Educators also joined the cause. Acting director of the Art Institute of Chicago, George William Eggers, issued a "Call to Service," in which he stated: "From this moment Art must exist no longer for Art's sake, but for the sake of the republic.... There are numberless ways in which our Art may be a handmaiden in the nation's service."

Eggers was by no means a lone voice. New York School of Fine and Applied Art faculty and students made posters for the Army and the National Guard. Courses in the creation of the war poster were begun in art schools and universities. This concern was but part of the rapidly heating public spirit.

In the one short year that had elapsed since the first meeting of the poster advertising community, local and regional efforts had become distinguished by an efficiency that exceeded even Barney Link's expectations.

When the Associated Advertising Clubs of the World met in St. Louis in June 1917, a Liberty Bond poster by James Montgomery Flagg greeted all comers. This mounted, twenty-four-sheet billboard dramatized the war mobilization effort, which, by the end of 1919, had resulted in more than 28,000,000 posters being produced for the Liberty Loan drives alone (100,000 of these were twenty-four-sheet posters). It is estimated that the outdoor industry gave more than $1.5 million in space to the cause.

The war was won, and with it the outdoor advertising industry and advertising agencies—now coming of age—won a level of acceptability that was possible only through this opportunity to merge a patriotic cause with long-term industry objectives.

This Liberty Bond poster by James Montgomery Flagg, creator of the famous *I Want You* Uncle Sam recruitment poster, greeted delegates to the convention of the Associated Advertising Clubs of the World, held in June 1917 in St. Louis.

James Montgomery Flagg with a model in front of the New York Public Library building, Fifth Avenue and Forty-Second Street, in the early summer of 1918.

Joseph C. Leyendecker's recruitment poster of 1917 draws on the all-American passion for baseball (30 x 20"). Joseph C. (not to be confused with his brother Francis X.) was to become one of America's best-known illustrators.

Right: A daunting Liberty urges the purchase of bonds in this undated 56 x 38" poster by John Scott Williams. Williams was best known for his magazine cover illustrations, murals, and stained-glass work.

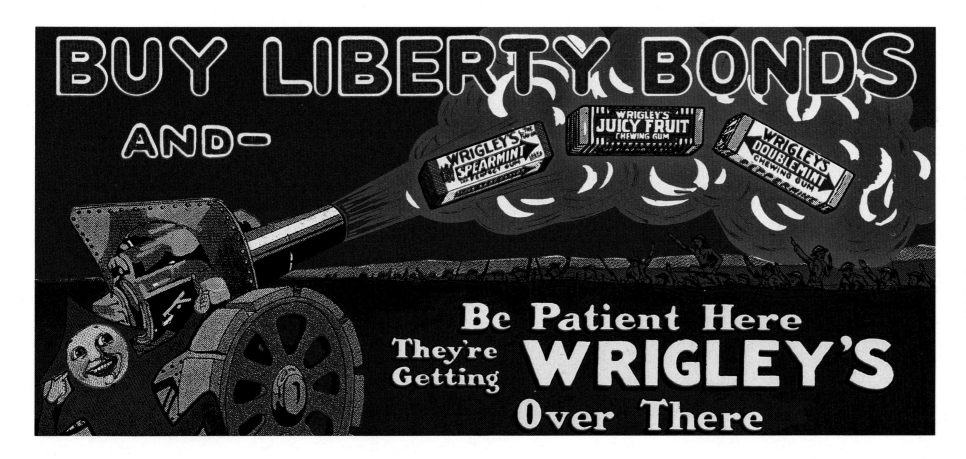

Wrigley's twenty-four-sheet *Buy Liberty Bonds* billboard (1919) was typical of World War I advertising that mixed public service with product promotion. Note the "spear person" in the lower left corner.

Left: Neysa Moran McMein's 1918 stylized Y.M.C.A. girl raises her cup to the allure of foreign travel and to the patriotism of war work (42 x 28"). McMein's war mobilization work helped launch her long career as a painter.

N. C. Wyeth was the second major American illustrator to prepare a billboard for Fisk tires (1919).

Overleaf, left: Bloch Brother's Tobacco Company introduced Mail Pouch chewing tobacco in 1897, and advertised it on barns and painted signs until the mid-teens, when they began to use billboards. This 1919 twenty-four-sheet example reflects the increased sophistication of the company's advertising by this time.

Overleaf, right: This 1919 Yucatan Gum poster prepared for the American Chicle Company is the earliest-known photographic twenty-four-sheet poster.

40

Members of the California Fruit Growers'
Exchange (founded in 1893) marketed
their citrus under the name of Sunkist
from the time the group began advertising
nationally, around 1910. C. A. Federer
was commissioned to paint the ideal
display of citrus products in this
grocer's shop (1919).

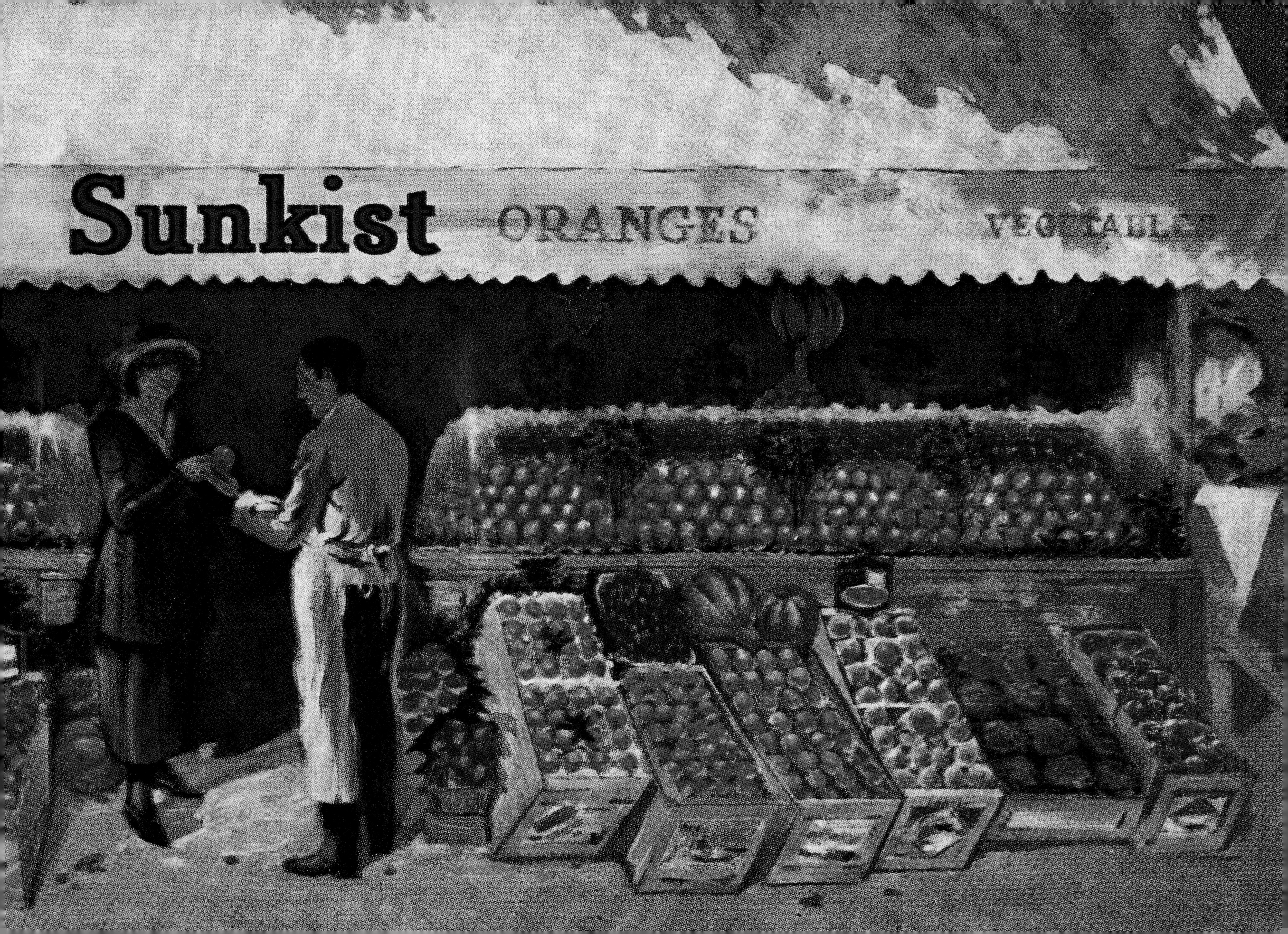
Sunkist
ORANGES

◆

THE GOLDEN AGE OF BILLBOARDS:
THE TWENTIES

With the signing of the Treaty of Versailles in 1919, the world looked quite bright for Americans. At least a certain degree of economic optimism was evident, despite what from this vantage looks like a quite questionable future. The country was in the throes of a Spanish flu epidemic that was to kill 500,000 Americans. (Only 126,000 had died in the war.) There was little concern here over the portent of European events in this signal year: Mussolini's founding of the Fasci di Combattimento, Hitler's creation of the National Socialist Worker's Party, and Lenin's establishment of the Comintern were but distant events of merely local concern. But even in Europe, few people among these three countries' neighbors saw these events as particularly ominous.

British war hero Sir John William Alcock and Arthur Brown were making the first nonstop flight across the Atlantic, United Artists was founded, and what Henry Ford was doing that year is part of American business lore. These three events were to have a far-reaching impact on American society, which was just awakening to the pleasures of leisure time—another business frontier for the new generation of entrepreneurs.

Without a wasted moment, America was building an economy oriented as no other in history to the manufacture of consumer goods in unrivaled variety.

World War I had provided outdoor advertisers with a laboratory for experimentation. Artists and illustrators saw the effects of synthesizing the newly perceived understanding of color, word, and image into persuasive, psychologically effective messages. This experience gave advertising executives (and politicians) a new kind of power. At war's end, the outdoor advertising industry had campaign ideas in place, ready to capitalize on the peacetime market as Americans rushed to put the war behind them.

Certainly, by every measurement, 1919 was the send-off year for poster and billboard advertising. According to the industry journal (renamed *The Poster*), it was "the best year that has ever been recorded in the history of the medium." American manufacturers were outdoing themselves in the variety of products offered and were moving to outdoor advertising in record numbers. Outdoor advertising companies began to expand their plants throughout the country in order to accommodate the burgeoning interest in and use of the billboard. Many installed their own art departments with skilled designers to serve local accounts more effectively.

The L. E. Waterman Company, for example, took the public service route. This pen manufacturer prepared a map-poster and waited for the announcement of the territorial demarcations determined by the Allies and the United States. With the news of the signing on June 28, 1919, came the signal for the presses to roll. Forty-eight hours later, the posters were ready for distribution and hanging, with their implied message of Waterman pens as instruments of peace.

Waterman was but one company committed to outdoor advertising as the result of its success with the medium in the first two decades of the century. Many others (or their successors) are still part of the American business scene: Wilson & Company (meat

packing); Bunte Brothers (candy); Hart, Schaffner & Marx (clothing); Champion Spark Plug Company; Standard Oil Company; Firestone Tire and Rubber Company; Calumet Baking Powder; California Fruit Growers' Exchange; Bloch Brothers (Mail Pouch tobacco); Channell Chemical Company (O-Cedar polish); American Tobacco Company (Lucky Strike); American Chicle Company; Fisk Rubber Company; Ansco Camera Company; Ford Motor Company; and Kodak.

Aside from these manufacturers who used the billboard, the twenties also saw the use of outdoor advertising by the growing leisure industry, particularly movie and tourist-related businesses. As numerous book-length studies have shown, the mass-produced automobile has had a greater effect on American culture, landscape, and outdoor advertising than any other single invention. The automobile was the essential element for billboard expansion. Once postwar production was under way, the automobile allowed the farmer (America was still over 50 percent rural in 1920), wife, and children to visit their trading center or other, larger towns with relative ease and frequency. The entire family could be offered products of the rapidly expanding economy via a tantalizing array of carefully designed inducements.

Retailers were discovering another means of expanding the market even faster: encouraging Americans to buy on time. Advertising directed at such large purchases as cars urged the public to pay as it rode. Installment buying would account for nearly $6 billion annually by the last years of the decade.

In the mid-twenties, the outdoor advertising industry was at last generally accepted by the banking community. New York's Outdoor Advertising Company was even listed on the New York Stock Exchange.

In 1921, the Federal Highway Act was passed in recognition that a national road system was essential to continuing economic development. Once again, events worked to the direct advantage of the ever-advancing outdoor advertising industry. With the advent of better and longer stretches of highway, billboards would offer a traveling captive audience refrigerators and food, vacations and clothes, and, of course, automobiles and their related products. Gasoline, batteries, tires (which had a road life of about 5,000 miles in 1919), and various accessories were all promoted to passing driv-

ers. It is not surprising that the producers of these items, particularly such tire manufacturers as Fisk, Goodyear, and Firestone, competed vigorously in their poster designs.

Fisk had managed to bring Maxfield Parrish, the best-known illustrator of the era, to the poster boards of America. Miss M. G. Webber, outdoor advertising manager for Fisk, had not had success in attracting major illustrators in the prewar period. But in 1916 Fisk made a conscious effort to restructure its approach with its "Art in Posters" campaign. This gave Miss Webber sufficient courage to call on Maxfield Parrish, who, apparently taken with her mission of aesthetic education and of "cultivating a wider liking for good pictures," agreed to a billboard commission. In a speech before the Poster Advertising Association's annual meeting in 1919, Miss Webber stated that attracting Parrish was the key to "unlocking every studio door we have since approached."

In that same year, a liaison was created between the Poster Advertising Association and the Association of National Advertisers. At the National Outdoor Convention in Atlantic City, George Chennell, chairman of the promotion committee, announced that the Association of National Advertisers (representing some $600 million in all advertising media) joined for the first time in making the billboard better known, thus adding further opportunities for expansion.

Movie posters, church posters, the first billboard designed to be read by pilots (over Chicago), European peacetime poster campaigns, war poster design from various countries, posters for developing aviation interests, and, of course, successful domestic product campaigns—these were but some of the issues and themes occupying the industry in the first year of the new decade. But balancing aesthetic improvement with commercial purpose remained foremost.

The advertising tie-in also grew in popularity, for it benefited both the manufacturer and the local merchant. A local billboard plant manager might be aware several weeks in advance of an upcoming national campaign—for raisins, for example. He would contact local raisin users (bakers, candy makers, and so on), encouraging them to create local poster advertising to run at the same time. Such a concept seems obvious to us now, but at that time it was revolutionary.

The L. E. Waterman Company had this twenty-four-sheet scoop ready within forty-eight hours of the armistice signing in 1919.

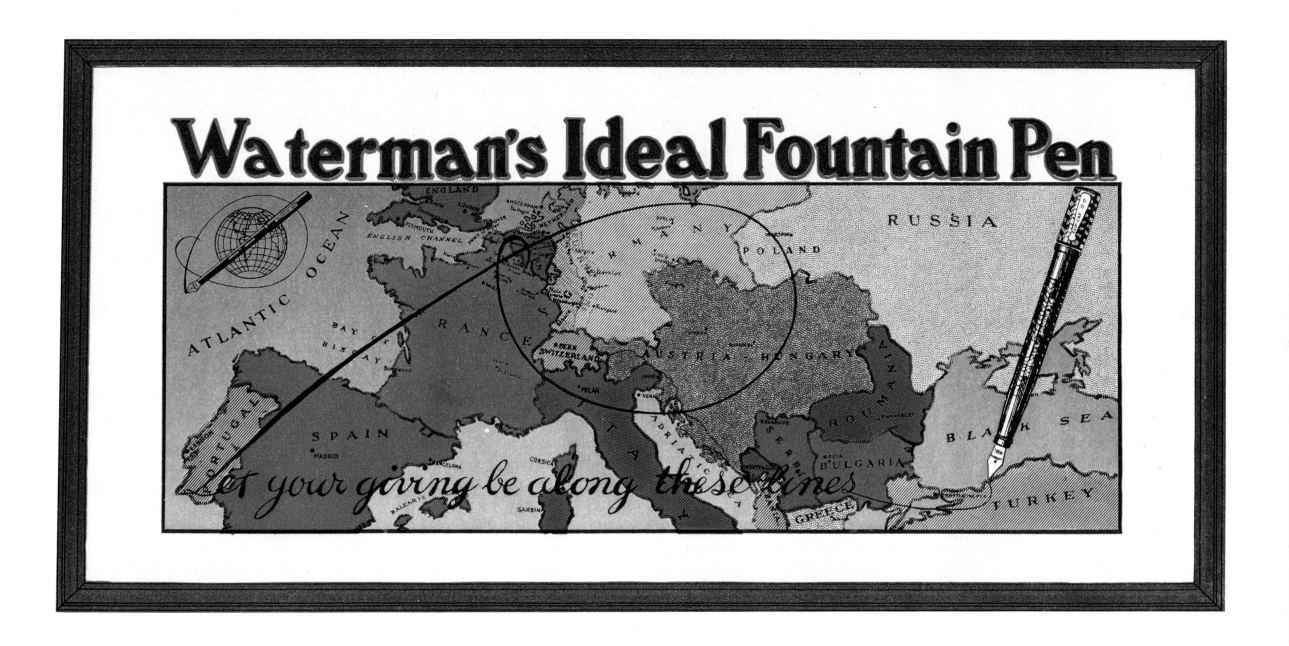

Effective distribution of consumer goods was a constant challenge, and the subject of at least one speaker's talk at nearly every outdoor advertising convention throughout the decade. The mechanics of distribution of goods was usually handled efficiently by rail over long as well as short distances. But erratic publication of advance promotional materials distributed by manufacturers to retail outlets created obvious problems for retailers—they often learned of new products from billboards or newspaper and magazine advertising.

In the twenties, the non–English-speaking and -reading minority was a sizable but easily forgotten market: several million immigrants were limited to their minority-language press for information. (In 1920, some 16,000,000 non-English readers amounted to 15 percent of the population.)

Since immigrants regularly sent money home, the U.S. Post Office Division of Money Orders was faced with a multilingual clientele. To rebuild business, which had fallen off during the war, the division began advertising its services in ten of the twenty-four foreign languages in which the post office regularly published informational material. Posters for this successful campaign were printed in Italian, Greek, Spanish, French, Polish, Hungarian, Lithuanian, Armenian, Portuguese, and Yiddish. Regional campaigns also used Finnish, Czech, Russian, Croatian, Slovak, Chinese, and Japanese. (Today's needs as perceived by the U.S. Postal Service are different; its only non-English posters are in Spanish.)

The patriotic message billboards and posters carried in the war years was not entirely subsumed by the commercial. In the early and mid-1920s, the industry continued its civic betterment efforts in some 10,000 towns across the country where Poster Advertising Association members had plants. This campaign consisted of "loyalty posters" promoting the Boy Scouts of America, the Girl Scouts, regular church attendance, traffic safety, and the like. This civic interest brought praise from both the local and national press: the outdoor advertising industry did have a conscience.

Mid-decade was an obvious time for a look back to the turn of the century. While the Poster Advertising Association had existed for thirty-four years, it was the first twenty-five years of this century that had seen such stellar development in what was now a major industry. (In 1900, for example, the total spent for regulated advertising outdoors was around $2 million. By 1925, this figure had reached $60 million, an increase of some 3,000 percent.)

Realistically, one could make this quarter-century outdoor advertising record even more impressive by considering that standardization, which gave the industry its strength, was not fully in place until 1912. After that point, standardized outdoor service was at the disposal of national advertisers in nearly every major urban center. This brought not only service, but an identifiable, well-maintained structure—an important element in attracting and maintaining advertisers. The green-framed billboard was available in some 14,000 cities and towns to carry images of Coca-Cola, Palmolive soap, and the products of William Wrigley, Jr., the National Biscuit Company, General Electric, and Ford. All of these firms credited outdoor advertising with their unprecedented growth in the twenties.

In 1925, the first major merger of outdoor advertising firms took place. For years, smaller companies had been bought and sold by slightly larger companies, but in this year, the so-called Fulton Group, a considerable number of modest-size companies, and the relatively large and well-known Thomas Cusack Company of Chicago combined to become the General Outdoor Advertising Company (GOA). This merger was a decided advantage to the merchandising and service information network of the American business community. Unifying a large number of smaller firms, many with years of experience serving specialized markets, created a more efficient network linking merchandisers, advertisers, and their geometrically expanded market contacts.

Tourism and such tourist-related service industries as hotels and restaurants were to benefit immeasurably from this consolidation. GOA's house organ regularly published the success stories of tourism expansion in the second half of the decade.

GOA was the giant of the eastern half of the country. It retained the best in-house artists, helping to set the tone for much of American advertising of the time. This tone was unfailingly conservative: company artists did not seem to be influenced by contemporary European design trends. Even the more modern look created by Southern California graphic designers of the period seemed to have little impact on this New York–based school.

Not until 1928 did the annual poster design entries from the

West Coast with their obvious references to the "new wave" receive attention in the design annuals of *The Poster*. The conservative clients, ad agencies, and outdoor advertising companies were having too much success to change, despite their apprehension about possible competition from a new medium—radio.

Even though the outdoor advertising industry had experienced sizable increases in revenue every year since the close of World War I, the fact that more than 5,000,000 shares of stock in fledgling radio manufacturing companies had changed hands was not reassuring. It was estimated that in 1925 there were already 2,500,000 receiving sets in use. A large percentage of these had been produced at home or in school shop classes. Even this fact was unsettling. When a new medium becomes part of the public school curriculum, it can only mean that it will be around for a while.

The outdoor advertising industry's response was to solicit radio promotion. Some manufacturers, such as David Grimes, used billboards to launch their product. Grimes preceded his campaign with a careful market study, resulting in four posters (for his initial series): the first, a teaser, "Please, Stand by—Wait for the New David Grimes Radio Receiving Set, a Sensation"; the second, an announcement, "It's here, the new David Grimes Radio Sensation" (along with a picture of a stork delivering the radio in a sling); the third, the "prestige copy," "The David Grimes Radio, a contribution to Civilization"; and, finally, the "sell," which simply shows the receiver and states "David Grimes Radio."

In his first twelve months, 1924–25, Mr. Grimes sold nearly 200,000 sets, primarily with outdoor advertising. But all the good equipment, good advertising, and goodwill could not keep the small, polite radio manufacturers such as Mr. Grimes in business for long in the scramble for market territory that ensued during the remainder of the decade. Grimes, Kellogg, Brunswick-Panatrope, Erla, and Splitdorf are now long forgotten; Atwater Kent is remembered vaguely by those who also recall the Cliquot Club Eskimos and the A & P Gypsies. Only RCA Radiola is alive, in another form, and remembered. These firms all used billboards as they struggled and lost—or, in the case of RCA, won.

Poor graphics might have been at fault for the downfall of these many radio companies, but it is unlikely. In those years, all radio companies used graphics that were comfortable, romantic, and little different from the furniture advertising of the time. None, not even RCA, sought a design approach commensurate with the extraordinary potential of this medium of the future with all its intangible qualities. A few posters and print advertisements had benign lightning bolts streaking from radio tower to receiver, but the settings were mainly twenties-cozy or little more than the radio itself with a neutral background. If the art directors or artists of the time were eager for more daring approaches, the audience was apparently perceived as being unready.

One can only speculate what the radio poster advertising (or any other poster advertising) of the 1920s might have been if, for example, E. McKnight Kauffer, the leading expatriate American poster maker, had not moved to England in 1915; if George Kleiser's encouragement of designers, art directors, and manufacturers to introduce the masses to European design trends had had more success; or if the Foster and Kleiser Outdoor Company had been located in New York instead of California.

The Foster and Kleiser plant at Third and San Pedro, Los Angeles, around 1920. At this time, the firm's artists were very much in tune with modern design trends, in contrast to many artists east of the Mississippi.

Right: In 1903, the Beatrice Creamery Company created the brand name Meadow Gold for a product the public was already buying. The name was designed to convey the idea of freshness as well as uniform quality and color, and was sufficiently convincing to sell in excess of 25,000,000 pounds annually by 1922, the date of this poster.

In all likelihood, it would not have made much difference. American manufacturers sold to a broad middle and lower middle class. Americans seemed to respond to realism; it sold products. It was and is the style that the broadest mass of Americans understand, according to the late Howard Scott, veteran billboard artist. In a conversation with the French poster designer A. M. Cassandre in 1939, Scott stated: "Exhaustive surveys have been made of the merits of our point of view—realistic posters—and they have proved conclusively that as far as America is concerned we are on the right track in putting on, as I like to call them, one-act plays to a five-second audience."

Who were the leading realist artists in the 1920s? Many, though previously successful, had come to positions of leadership in the art community as the result of their World War I poster successes—James Montgomery Flagg, C. B. Falls, Adolph Treidler, Howard Chandler Christy, Gordon Grant, Edward Blashfield, Jack Sheridan, Ernest Hamlin Baker, Herbert Paus, Walter Whitehead, Fred G. Cooper, J. C. Leyendecker, Norman Rockwell. Other noted artists and illustrators from the first two decades of the century who had contributed to the war effort—such as Harrison Fisher, James Daugherty, Arnold Genthe, Jessie Willcox Smith, Charles Dana Gibson, and Voitech Preissig—went back to what they were doing before the war and produced only occasional posters, if any, during the twenties. Daugherty became lost in what he called "synchronist abstractions," moving later into children's book illustration. Genthe continued his pursuit of photography. Jessie Willcox Smith was kept busy producing cover after cover for *Good Housekeeping*, as well as many book and magazine illustrations.

Clarence Underwood, certainly one of the most sought-after billboard artists of the decade, became something of a star. His Palmolive women and Camel men sold unprecedented quantities of the two products, along with the illusions of youth and masculinity. Underwood was imitated by numerous lesser artists who tried to achieve for their clients something of the success in the market for which he was known.

The new names in billboard art in the 1920s had either been students in the previous decade or were individuals who saw the distinct advantage of moving into advertising because of the increasing demand for commercial artists in this time of economic expansion. Haddon Sundblom, Charles S. Chapman, Thomas Benrimo, John O'Neill, Dorothy Hope Smith, A. Von Frankenburg, Denman Fink, and Jon Brubaker are but a few who became well known in this and the following decade. Ludwig Hohlwein, the noted Munich poster artist, took his first billboard commission in the United States (for Fatima cigarettes) in 1925. (Hohlwein had been working for American clients as early as 1910, when he created a single-sheet poster to promote Yellowstone Park; in 1912, he created one for the Wonalancet Company of Nashua, New Hampshire, a textile equipment manufacturer.)

A major event in the history of American advertising art took place in 1920, when the Art Directors Club was organized in New York City. The specialized activity, even predating the war, of advising business in the use of art for furthering its goals had brought into being a specialist, the "art director" (the term came into general use in the second decade of the century). What the founding of such an organization meant for commercial art was the establishment of standards through competitions and the identification of categories of commercial art endeavor.

Billboard designers have been club members since the organization's founding; many have been members of the annual exhibition committees. Posters have often been included in the club's exhibitions, and many of those selected for awards or honorable mention were designed specifically for the outdoors. In general, these winning posters reflected the philosophy of Harold Scott, quoted above. Few would argue with the choices in the first Art Directors Annual Exhibition: the first award was given to René Clarke, and honorable mentions went to Elizabeth Shippen Green Elliott, Edward Penfield, and Adolph Treidler. Only Clarke, who lived until 1969, went on to major achievements in subsequent decades. He may have been the only designer in history to give a can of cooking oil (Wesson) something approaching elegance. (Clarke was one of eight to be chosen for the Art Directors' Hall of Fame when it was created, in 1971.)

As mentioned previously, what is noteworthy about this decade, in which graphic design worldwide was anything but static, is that the outdoor advertising community and the art directors serving it continued to rely on realism despite the shoulder rubbing that must have gone on at the Art Directors Annual Exhibition.

These 1924 billboard painters were on location on Pico Boulevard in west Los Angeles. Their cars carried all essentials—brushes, paints, and other tools of the trade.

A "pilaster" lighted billboard structure in Los Angeles around 1925. The pilaster boards, referred to as "lizzies" in the trade, were created by Foster and Kleiser, the leading West Coast outdoor advertising firm, as a means of "upgrading the neighborhood." The structures were in use from 1923 to 1931, when maintenance costs forced the company to discontinue their use.

Regardless of the changes that were becoming increasingly apparent in periodical, package, and promotional materials design, the general outdoor industry view at the time was that highly stylized design or the "European influence" was fine for periodical advertising where text can expand upon the design. But since a billboard has only a few seconds to convey its message in image and text—unless it is designed to leave a question in the mind of the viewer such as "Are my tires unsafe?"—it should remove any guessing from the viewer's mind as to the product's utility, importance, or life-changing capacity. Thus, the outdoor poster designers stayed with the direct, realistic approach.

seemed to rely more heavily on airbrushing as well. It is instructive to compare year by year the work of the giant of the East, General Outdoor Advertising of New York, with that of Foster and Kleiser, the giant of the West and portions of the mountain states. We can see that there were two perceptions of the mass market: on the West Coast, stylization was sometimes effective, but in the East and Midwest, only realism "sold."

This gap gradually closed toward the end of the decade, and one might postulate that the Art Directors Annual Exhibition was a prime factor. In a decade, it had become an institution of some force in the advertising community, and the profession of art director was firmly established.

Poster contests and poster education, helping the public "read" the medium, have remained part of the outdoor industry policy in some form even to the present. Extending education efforts to sensitize the coming generation to the poster as a medium took the form of institutionalizing poster-design contests in elementary and high schools throughout the country. The legendary Harry O'Mealia of O'Mealia Outdoor Advertising, a forerunner of United Outdoor (now absorbed by Gannett Outdoor), was an unrelenting proponent of school poster art competitions throughout his lifetime. Although school poster contests have had an uneven history in the post–World War II period, O'Mealia kept the idea alive and thriving in New Jersey. Today, Gannett Outdoor continues to sponsor an annual statewide poster contest through the art departments of New Jersey high schools.

In 1925, the Poster Advertising Association and the Painted Outdoor Advertising Association joined to become the Outdoor Advertising Association of America, the name the association carries to this day. Its journal, *The Poster*, a mirror of the industry's hopes, fears, and dreams, became a victim of economic problems in 1930, when its name was changed to *Advertising Outdoors*. Color covers and color illustrations were dropped. Fewer articles on the history and aesthetics of the poster were run, and a decidedly businesslike tone suddenly prevailed.

In some ways, *The Poster* closed the decade as well as a period in which a more leisurely approach to marketing prevailed. As the industry entered the 1930s, the rather stark, stylized cover for the January 1930 issue of its journal foreshadowed the new era.

This is not to say that throughout the twenties billboard art was all of a piece. This would be amply clear to anyone looking at the work being done by the in-house artists of the Foster and Kleiser Company in San Francisco and Los Angeles. Such artists as C. Maurice Mayer, Leonard B. Hamshaw, Karl Koch, Wallace Harrison, J. Asanger, Arnold Armitage, William Stevens, Sonia Judson, and Maurice Del Mue were very much in tune with those modern design trends, moving to the stylized. These artists were also introducing softer but brighter colors not in the palette of the majority of those artists working for clients east of the Mississippi. They

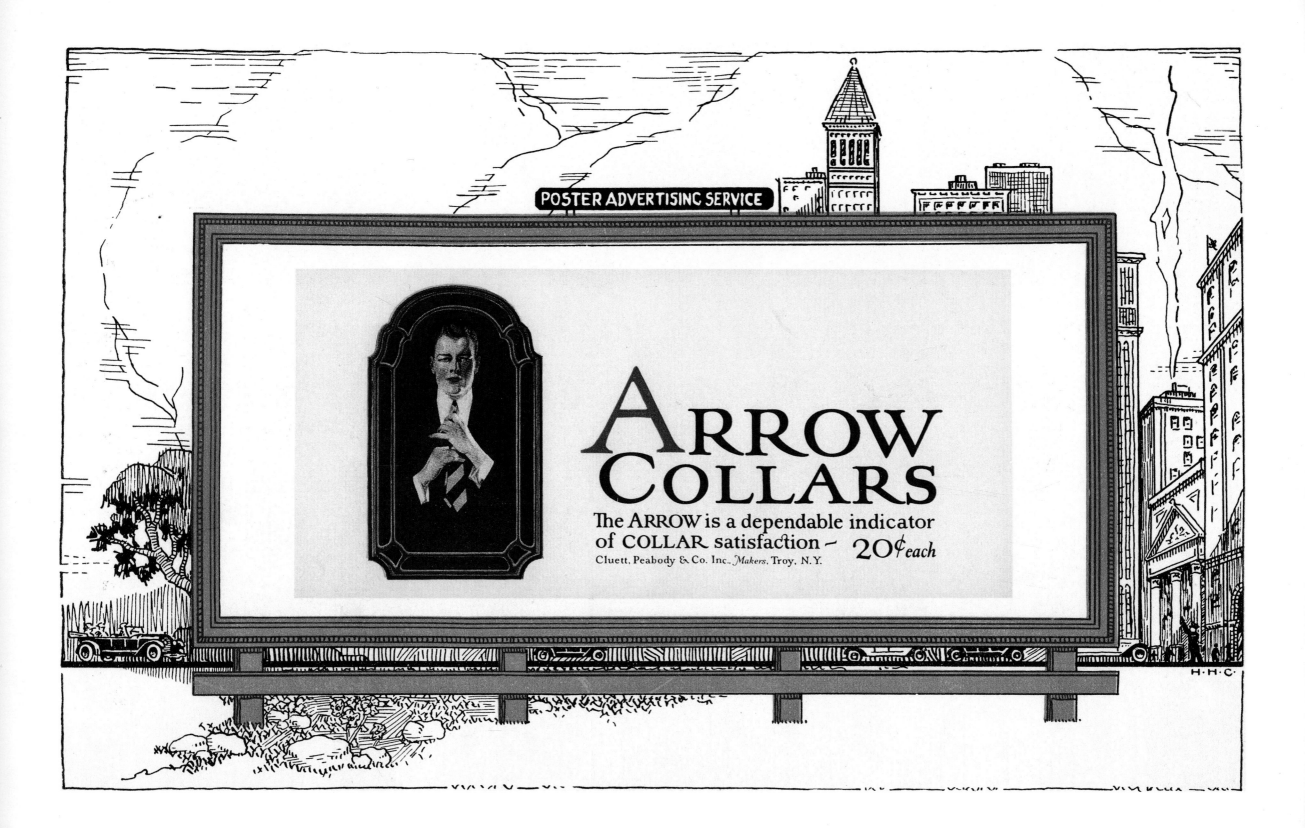

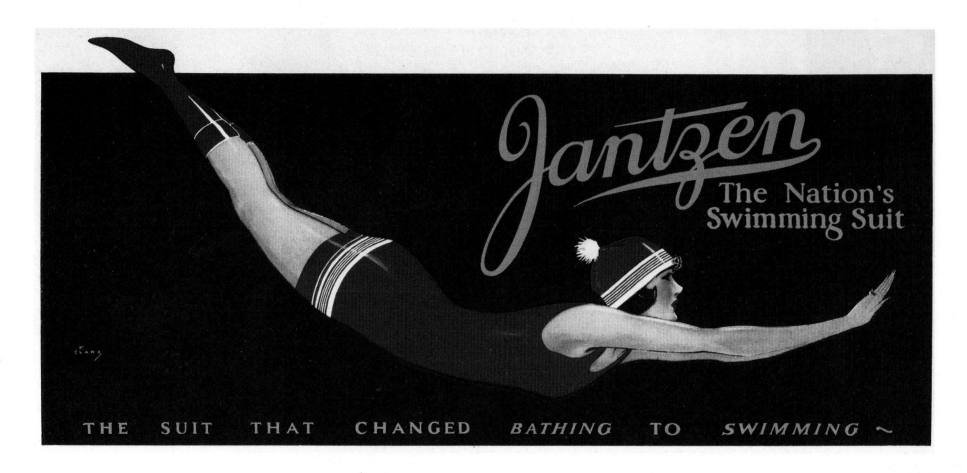

Frank and Florence Clark, who created the original Jantzen diving girl in 1916, were responsible for this 1924 depiction as well, even though the renowned illustrator McClelland Barclay had been commissioned to paint her by 1922.

Left: In merchandising their most up-to-date collars, Cluett-Peabody took advantage of the power of point-of-purchase advertising by employing the designs of Joseph C. Leyendecker. Billboards like these were placed near haberdashery shops as a final reminder to buy.

Above: The Moon Motor Car Company of St. Louis produced quality automobiles from 1905 to 1930. During the 1920s, the company's advertising was noted for its uncluttered style.

Below: Lincoln Motorcar Company (founded in 1920) and other manufacturers of the period relied upon landscape and strong but dignified typography to convey gentility and the authority of status conferred by driving a luxury automobile (1924).

Right: The U.S. Tire "book boards" were a fixture on American roadways from 1917, when the idea was introduced, until maintenance costs forced them to be discontinued in the late 1930s. Some structures remained standing in Western and Midwestern states as late as the 1940s. The illustration shown here, from an O. J. Gude promotion, appeared around 1926.

Ivory Soap made its first trademarked appearance in 1879 (the 99 44/100% pure slogan didn't appear until 1882). By the early 1920s, Procter & Gamble was a convinced billboard user. The company commissioned such major illustrators as Andrew Loomis, who created these posters in 1927.

This travel poster by Arnold Armitage (c. 1927) is typical of the highly stylized painted billboards being produced by the Foster and Kleiser Company in the late 1920s.

Above: Walter Dorwin Teague's *Aristocracy in Motor Cars* was designed in 1927 for a twenty-four-sheet poster, although it was not known to have been produced with text for a specific client. Teague had moved from rather fussy cartouche designs for such clients as Locomobile, Bulova Watch, and West Virginia Pulp and Paper to this more stylized approach by the end of the twenties.

Below: Originally from Germany, Jacob Asanger was brought to the West Coast from New York by George Kleiser in the mid-1920s. His 1928 design shown here, although not produced as a billboard, was used in the industry's 1928 publication *Outdoor Advertising—The Modern Marketing Force*. Asanger often designed frames and structures that were tied in their design to the copy and illustrations of his poster. Only a few such integrated creations were produced, however, because of cost.

Right: W. L. Jacoby, president of Kellogg Switchboard and Supply Company (Chicago), departed from a strictly realistic approach for his 1929 radio campaign by using a portrait style for a series of three billboards. G. Reid and Fred Gray painted the series and won honorable mention for this billboard in the 1930 Best Posters of the Year competition.

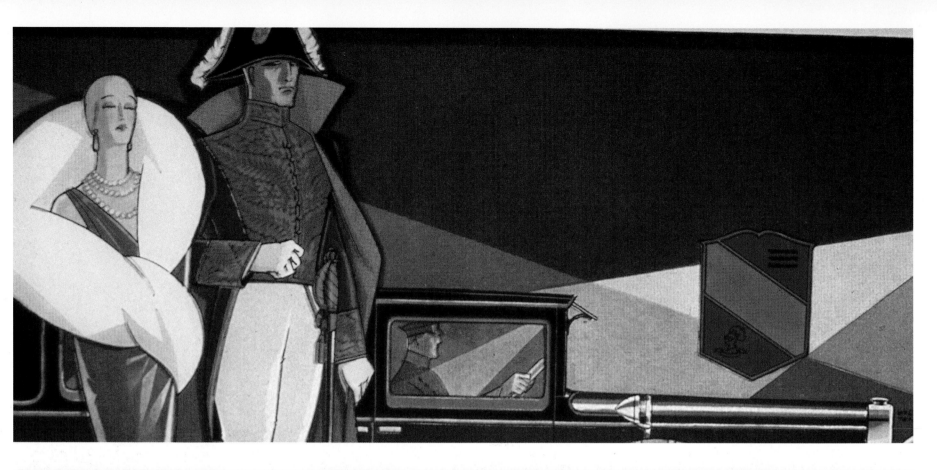

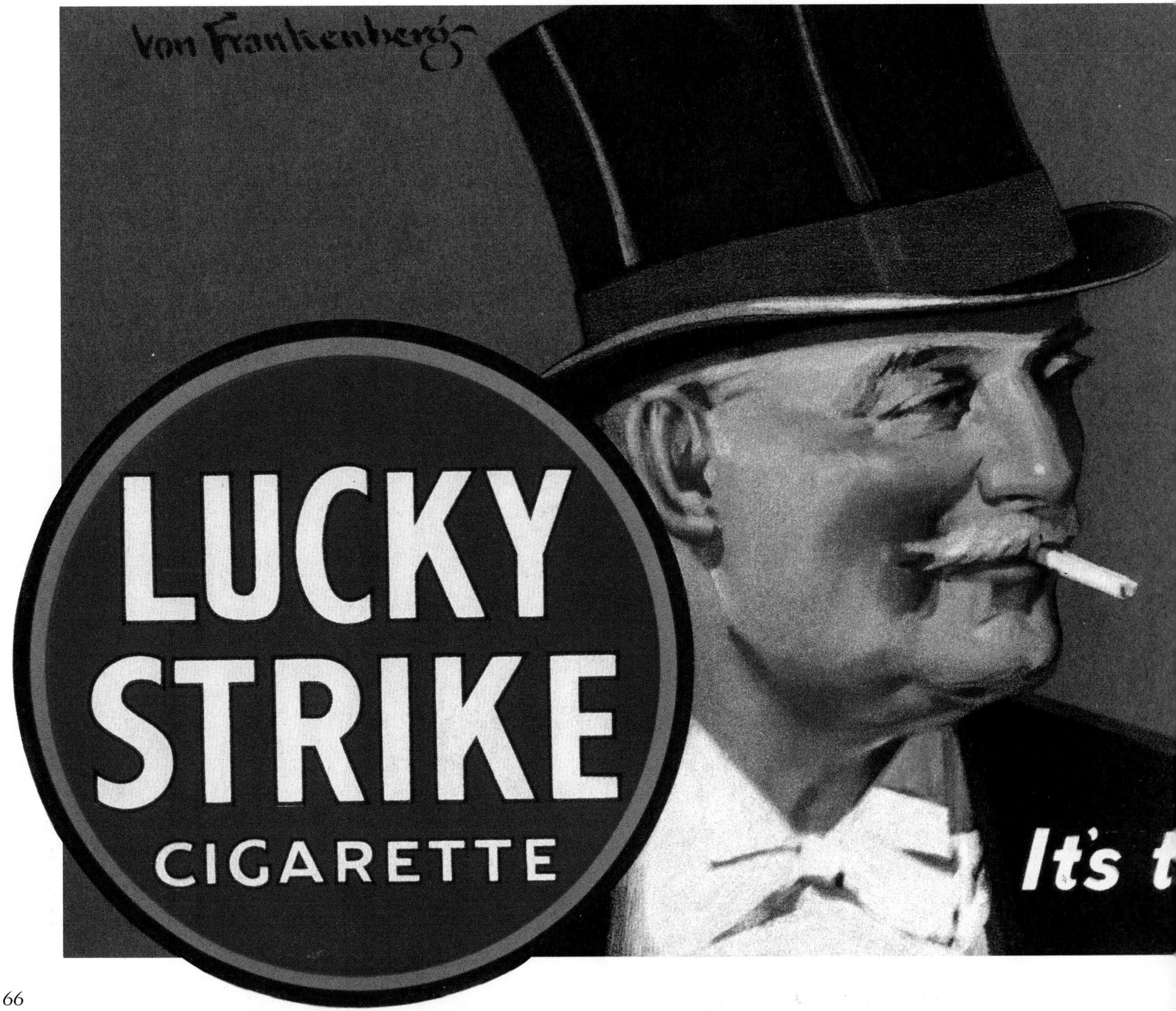
von Frankenberg
LUCKY STRIKE
CIGARETTE
It's t

These pink-cheeked gents celebrate the joys of Lucky Strikes in this 1925 billboard by L. von Frankenberg, about whom very little—including his first name—is known.

THE BRIGHTER SIDE OF THE DEPRESSION: THE THIRTIES

"the RITZ James!" by George Brehm received honorable mention in the 1937 100 Best Posters competition.

Mention the 1930s in the 1980s and for most visually literate Americans, the faces and tumbledown buildings of Walker Evans photographs come immediately to mind. The Great Depression is a phrase that evokes further bleak images of life in America. And it was bleak. Though most large manufacturers made noble attempts at selling, Americans were struggling to get by with what they had; most who were able to buy anything at all were unable to afford anything but the essentials. There was much leisure time for the unemployed, and the film industry managed to relieve some of the painful day-to-day reality for some of the population.

But the outdoor advertising industry and its employees did not have quite as much time for leisure as the rest of the population. Outdoor advertising was one of the few growth industries of the time, thanks to the inspired idea of the industry leaders who, on Friday, March 13, 1931, formed Outdoor Advertising, Inc. This new agency was founded to place "at the disposal of advertisers and agencies all the cooperation and facilities needed to develop a wider, more intelligent, and more profitable use of outdoor advertising." In contrast to the National Outdoor Advertising Bureau, with its primary concern with buying outdoor advertising and inspecting for compliance, the OAI was mainly concerned with selling the concept of outdoor advertising. It worked.

In 1932, there were 352 users of outdoor advertising nationwide with a total volume of sales of $20 million. The next year, this had grown to 482 users with a $33.6 million volume, and by 1939, 520 companies were expanding the medium's volume to $36.37 million. The industry was growing. No bankruptcies occurred, although many plants scaled down their operations to half or less.

The creation of Outdoor Advertising, Inc., was not the only innovation of the time. For a number of years, national advertisers, advertising agencies, and the industry, of course, had been concerned about the need for a system to measure the audience passing a given billboard site. A research fund at the University of Wisconsin, established in 1924 in the name of Barney Link, one of the major figures in the field in the first quarter of the century, was used to conduct primary research on this subject. In 1931, the University of Wisconsin published a study, *A Method of Making Short Traffic Counts and Estimating Traffic Circulation in Urban Areas*, which provoked further research sponsored by the industry and conducted at Harvard University. Following these studies, which consisted of traffic audits in more than 150 cities around the United States, a set of basic principles was established for measuring the audience of outdoor advertising. In February 1934, the industry established the Traffic Audit Bureau, to provide advertisers with the necessary data for determining the size of the audience viewing its billboards. The bureau, which serves the same role for the outdoor industry and its advertisers that the Nielsen ratings do for the television industry, has grown from a manual process to a highly sophisticated operation in the 1990s.

While the marketing advances and market measuring innovations of the thirties may have been invisible to the public, what they could see probably raised their spirits—or at least that was the

intent. Billboards certainly did not reflect economic or social despair or upheaval. A look through the industry's poster annuals and the Art Directors Club annuals of the decade confirms this.

The 1930 annual *Advertising Outdoors* shows ninety-five designs. Of these, twenty-two are for travel or contain images of activities or goods associated with leisure time. Seventeen billboards advertise such luxury items as tobacco, chewing gum, or evening clothes for men. Twenty attempt to sell essentials, e.g., foodstuffs, soap, or toothpaste. The remainder—almost half of the billboards—are for gasoline and automobile-related items, miscellaneous products, or services.

The posters represented in the Art Directors Club annual for the same year break down similarly, but with an even greater proportion of luxury items being offered.

The Great Depression seemed far away in 1930, judging from these annuals.

By 1935, however, the Depression was a stark reality, but the pages of the *100 Best Posters* (the new name of the industry's annual) are still relatively cheery. Automobiles, swimsuits, beer, cigarettes, and soft drinks (mainly Coca-Cola) dominate. One does note a hint of conservation subtly presented, particularly in automotive products. Economy measures are implied in posters promoting the use of electricity, as well. Dependability is a theme of a number of posters.

Only one billboard indicates that all might not have been well in our society, and its message is relevant to almost any period. That poster, for the Citizens Family Welfare Committee (place unknown), shows an arm around someone obviously in difficulty. The text reads: "Lend a hand, neighbor."

The posters of this year, in which 10.5 million Americans were unemployed, still did not reflect social crisis in either text or image. Neither is the "hard sell" more in evidence in this difficult time than in any other, as some chroniclers of poster history have maintained. One new trend, though, is the increasing use of humor. Cartoons and caricatures feature in eight billboards; even Mickey Mouse appears selling Post Toasties for the General Foods Corporation. Only one caricature had appeared in the 1930 annual. The award-winning poster in the Art Directors exhibition for 1935 was decidedly in the "gentle humor" category, with a shorn lamb

pursued by a running bear and taunting the bear to "get Ethyl (gasoline)" next time.

Despite such well-known photographers as Edward Steichen, Anton Bruehl, Valentino Sarra, Grancel Fitz, and Margaret Bourke-White at work in mid-thirties advertising, the posters in the annuals do not indicate any particular dependence on photography, although two ads in the *100 Best Posters* do use photographs as the principal part of the illustration. By contrast, photography had already taken hold in magazine advertising by 1930; thirty-one of the 300 entries in the *Annual of Advertising Art* that year were photographs (and more than just a product close-up). Given the billboard advertisers' enthusiasm for realism, it seems strange that they were slow to embrace this technology.

In 1937, the year A. M. Cassandre's fabled *Watch the Fords Go By* received honorable mention, humor and the use of caricature and cartoon increased considerably. Six billboards had a humorous line or allusion, and fifteen posters were based on caricature or cartoon figures. Photography still fared poorly in 1937.

The year 1939 gave increasing hope to the outdoor advertising

This disembodied hand gripping the looming glass of Coca-Cola against a panoramic background was painted by N. C. Wyeth in 1937. The artist had created billboards for Coca-Cola in 1935 and 1936 as well.

Left: Otis Shepard received first prize in the Outdoor Advertising Association contest for this 1932 poster for Wrigley. By this time, Shepard had become widely known for his sophisticated "European-style" posters.

Overleaf, left: Andrew Loomis received honorable mention in the 1932 OAA awards for this General Electric refrigerator billboard. In 1932 alone, Loomis also had commissions from Iodent, Shell Motor Oil, Shell Gasoline, Sunkist, and Dr. Pepper.

Overleaf, right: The stylized approach in this 1933 billboard for a Portland, Oregon, client of Foster and Kleiser, was typical of the work of Karl Koch.

industry and Americans in general. But no sooner had the Depression run its course than certain ominous events occured in Europe. In 1939, German troops entered Czechoslovakia and Poland; Hitler and Mussolini signed their ten-year Pact of Steel; Italy invaded Albania; Britain and France declared war on Germany. Because most of the world-changing events took place in the second half of the year, when advertising schedules were already underway, one sees little concern reflected in billboard content. The visual idioms noted in mid-decade continued. The Art Directors' Kerwin H. Fulton Medal for the best twenty-four-sheet billboard went to Albert Staehle for his whimsical design for Essolene: *Spring Power*, in which a leaping frog dominates the poster in flight toward a lily pad. (Perhaps Staehle did have a darker, symbolic message in this image, an allusion to the unprecedented refugee flight taking place in that year.)

The number of posters included in the Art Directors show increased markedly in 1939, and with good reason. In addition to some of the well-known poster artists long identified with the industry (such as Staehle, Howard Scott, McClelland Barclay, Hayden Hayden, and Otis Shepard), the renowned Austrian designer Joseph Binder had left Vienna in 1933 to teach in the United States and was already sufficiently integrated into American advertising to have six of the twenty-six posters in this eighteenth annual exhibition. Stanley Ekman, Sascha Maurer, and Fred Ludekens are represented as well, bringing their stylized design to the billboard audience. Only six of the twenty-six posters rely on a realistic style, and one employs photography.

This diminishing number of realistic posters had already become evident the previous year, indicating at least a temporary move toward what many persisted in calling the European approach to poster design. Joseph Binder's influence may have been one factor. He and Otis Shepard (whose acknowledged debt to Binder was substantial) were widely watched at that time because of Binder's success in the Midwest as a teacher and Shepard's visibility as a consistent award winner. Both Shepard's Wrigley posters and Binder's work for Ballantine Ale and Beer are classic examples of 1930s airbrush artistry. Binder's prizewinning poster for the 1939 New York World's Fair only extended his influence as advertisers could not help but notice the triumph of the symbolic over

A 1939 photograph of the Foster and Kleiser art department, where so many great billboards were born. The artists (front to back): Jacob Asanger, Charles Austin, Edwin Fairbrother, Arnold Armitage, Al Teteak. Not shown: Lumir Matheuser.

Left: Joseph Binder received first prize in the McCandlish Poster Competition (Philadelphia, 1938) for this entry. Another Binder Ballantine poster was chosen in this same year in the 100 Best Posters competition.

Overleaf, left: Marshall Reid received first prize in the billboard industry's 1930 Best Posters of the Year competition for this Oxydol poster. Reid was also represented this same year by work for Butter-Nut Coffee, Silver Flash Gasoline, and Shellane Gas.

Overleaf, right: Howard Scott's prizewinning poster of 1931 reflects the trend toward simple humor that expanded throughout the 1930s and continued into the late 1950s.

the realistic in the response of Binder's growing audience.

In the late thirties, the trend away from folksy realism did not reflect only the wishes of a small circle of New York, Chicago, and Los Angeles designers. The decision-making public could not avoid responding to the new look of, for example, *Fortune Magazine* (with its articles on industrial and graphic design) or *Harper's Bazaar* with Alexey Brodovitch's soaring success in redesigning it in his new role as art director. House organs such as *More Business* or printing trades magazines such as *PM* pushed yet other constituencies toward the inevitable acceptance of the new style.

The New Poster International Exhibition, mounted at the Franklin Institute in Philadelphia in 1937, was in its own way a force in acquainting yet another circle of individuals, including billboard users, with the possibilities of the new design. The ostensible purpose of the exhibition was to show "current phases of foreign poster advertising, and to emphasize the artistic value of these tendencies to America poster design." The individuals involved were, as could be expected, a vanguard group: renowned art director Charles T. Coiner; Christian Brinton, the leading organizer of pre–World War I European art exhibitions in America; Alexey Brodovitch, chairman and designer of the exhibition and art director of *Harper's Bazaar*; A. M. Cassandre, the widely acknowledged leader

EX-LAX

This undated, anonymous Ex-Lax poster was produced in the 1930s by the Foster and Kleiser art department. It is typical of the 1930s trend of using photography in advertising in a direct fashion, although this approach was infrequently employed with billboards.

Left: Xanti Schawinsky created this poster maquette for the New Poster International Exposition, held in 1937 at the Franklin Institute in Philadelphia. The exhibition's purpose was to show the strength of symbolism and partial abstraction in conveying a message. Before coming to the United States in 1936, Schawinsky had made a few posters for such commercial clients as Olivetti in Milan. Once in the U.S., he made even fewer, alas, though he did work for the Citizens Housing Council of New York and Pan American Airways.

Overleaf, left: Despite the obvious high quality of design in this 1930 Bradley bathing suit poster, it was not selected for inclusion in the Best Posters of the Year exhibition.

Overleaf, right: George Petty of pin-up calendar and *Esquire* fame did several billboards for Jantzen in the 1930s and later. This is one of several from 1938.

of modern poster design; Joseph and Carla Binder; Xanti Schawinsky, former Bauhaus instructor; Sascha Maurer, a leading poster designer; and many others. The list of corporate sponsors, most of whom used outdoor advertising, is equally interesting in that few were consistent in their use of vanguard design: Autocar Company, Bonwit Teller, E. I. DuPont, Philco Radio, RCA, Sun Oil, and John Wanamaker.

Christian Brinton, in his essay for the catalogue, summed up what many in the outdoor advertising industry acknowledged—that many industry leaders had long since recognized the new wave, but they were reluctant to use it because of a perceived resistance on the part of the majority of consumers. Brinton stated that the "poster . . . epitomizes, as no other art form, the technique [style] of modern life." The posters in this turning-point exhibition bore this out dramatically: one need only look at Herbert Matter's poster for John Wanamaker; Lester Beall's for the Philadelphia Gas Works; Xanti Schawinsky's for Philco; Alexey Brodovitch's for the Pennsylvania State Police; or Lucian Bernhard's for Philco, to cite

but a few of the American entries.

But this exhibition and all the avant-garde design "in the air" didn't seem to make a lasting impact. Very little seeped down or out into the outdoor advertising industry as a whole.

By 1940, the industry's *100 Best Posters* showed no stylized symbols, but what one might call stylized realism *was* there. Again, one saw it mainly in the work of Joseph Binder, Otis Shepard, Sascha Maurer (his poster for Utah Oil Refining), Tom Ryan (his work for Los Angeles Brewing Company), and John Vickery (his posters for Best Foods). The rest is much as before, with the increasingly tedious humor relieved only by the whimsy of William Steig and his now-legendary *Shell Service Ahead* series.

Some might say that the thirties closed with the billboard industry having missed its opportunity to raise the general standard of graphic design in the country. The fact is, though, that many in the industry were ready, as were increasing numbers of art directors, but the public was not. As will be seen in subsequent chapters, it did not become ready until the 1960s and early 1970s.

In 1937, Dorothy Shepard received OAA's third award for this design, which has a surprisingly contemporary look. Three of her other Pabst posters were also selected in the same year.

THE 1940S: BACK TO WAR

I t was not until the shock of the Japanese attack on Pearl Harbor that American businesses began to realize that changes and challenges greater than the Depression were in store.

"Like many other businesses, the outdoor industry was immediately faced with panic-inspiring problems," Joe Blackstock, veteran industry historian, explains. "The prospect of rationing and curtailment of production of automobiles, tires, gasoline, food, and other outdoor-advertised products would likely affect the client list of every outdoor plant operator." Ad cancellations did indeed pour in during the early months of 1942, but, Blackstock continues, "As with most worrying, most of the more serious catastrophes never materialized. A variety of new and old advertisers kept plants busy throughout the war years. Most companies were able to retain or replace absent workers, and outdoor audiences remained remarkably stable despite fuel rationing." Share-the-ride outdoor advertising campaigns helped raise load factor in cars and mass transit.

America was on the move and outdoors as never before. In the forties, billboards were given high marks by virtually every constituency in American life—government, business, and the public sector. Outdoor advertising plants were besieged with requests for war service space, especially from the federal government, and city, county, and state governments not only wanted free promotional space, but they also needed special panels built at city halls and parks where war bond rallies and other patriotic meetings were being held.

Faced with wartime shortages of wood, steel, paper, gasoline, and manpower, billboard companies were often able to get high priorities to obtain such materials for war-oriented use. "Some outdoor plants provided camouflage for both civilian and military installations—and even some for use by military forces in the South Pacific," adds Blackstock. "Outdoor artists proved remark-ably adept at fulfilling such needs. Many firms built ammunition boxes and bricks for anti-aircraft gun revetments, as well as other war construction projects."

For this war, America was better organized. At least the outdoor advertising industry and the National Association of Manufacturers were ready with a variety of posters reminding Americans that "Industry is Producing for your Defense," pointing out that production of war materiel would ultimately have to take priority over consumer goods, and encouraging everyone to do the best possible in the face of shortages.

USO billboard campaigns and local and regional campaigns on the themes proposed by the National Association of Manufacturers were preliminary to the major campaigns that developed at the close of 1942 and continued throughout the remainder of the war.

On December 1, 1942, the Office of Civilian Defense launched a major campaign in cooperation with the outdoor-advertising industry to be used throughout the country dealing with various aspects of civilian defense. The first poster, Chester Miller's *Let 'em come . . . 'V' Homes are ready! Make yours a 'V' Home Now!*, evokes the right amount of fear to marshal the concerned parent to participate in the several phases of civil defense education and the steps for preparedness.

The next year marked a decided increase in poster activity related to the war effort both in governmental efforts and within the outdoor industry. In March, the industry put 17,000 poster panels at the disposal of the American Red Cross for its 1943 War Fund campaign. The design chosen was a painting by Lawrence Wilbur, *The Greatest Mother in the World*, the theme of a similar campaign in World War I. With this campaign, the Red Cross received the most complete coverage ever by the billboard industry. The largest previous campaign had not exceeded 5,200 posters. In addition to the initial 17,000 copies, 4,000 were produced for indepen-

This design by Hayden Hayden, c. 1943, is one of 105 billboards in the archival portfolio of twenty-four-sheet War Effort Mobilization Campaign posters designed and mounted by the billboard industry during World War II. The artists in the collection are as varied as Hayden Hayden and Joseph Binder, and many of the billboards are anonymous.

dent structures throughout the country and 2,000 more for special window displays in large department stores.

In April, the U.S. Treasury opened its Second War Loan drive with a goal to raise $13 billion. This particular campaign was a phenomenon in its own way, for its goal of raising this amount in just three weeks meant calling on every medium possible to reach into even the most isolated villages in the country. The poster designed by Marshall Reid for the campaign is simply a pennant with the inscription "Second War Loan" and text above and below it: "An investment for every purse. They give their lives—you lend your money." This poster, and presumably other efforts and mediums, resulted in the goal being met. In retrospect, the Treasury Department posters of that period were not generally inspiring, although Charles D. Jarrett's illustration incorporated into a 1942 war bond drive poster asking the country to "Save at Least 10% in War Bonds" must have helped in meeting that goal.

Other campaigns of 1942 included the War Manpower campaign to encourage those not in military or defense service to "Get a War Job to Help Him Fight!" The War Production Board continued urging Americans to save metal through its "junk campaign" posters. With the threat and success of Japanese incendiary balloons in the Pacific Northwest, the U.S. Department of Agriculture opened a Forest Fire Prevention Campaign in 1943 featuring a caricature of a Japanese military officer as well as Hitler on a twenty-four-sheet billboard reminding the reader: *Our Carelessness, Their Secret Weapon*. In the background, a forest is in flames.

This was also the spring in which the Department of Agriculture, in cooperation with the Office of Civilian Defense, used single-sheet posters as well as twenty-four-sheet billboards to promote the planting of victory gardens in many cities throughout the country. The operators of local billboard plants made land available for victory gardens adjacent to these posters. In a timely sequence to the April release of the victory garden campaign, in June, the Office of Civilian Defense released its *Add to Your Ration by Home Canning*. National policy encouraged each family to grow as much food as possible, and outdoor advertising at the national and local level reinforced this effort.

On September 9, 1943, the Third War Loan campaign was opened with 30,000 posters bearing a photo of Franklin Roosevelt stating, "As Commander-in-Chief, I hereby invoke every citizen to give all possible aid and support to the Third War Loan Drive."

By the end of the year, the outdoor advertising industry had contributed nearly $22.5 million worth of posters to various phases of the war effort. This extensive involvement of the industry in education, publicity, and recruitment extended right up to the end of the war and continued into the years of readjustment following it.

Generally speaking, the graphic design of the posters connected with the various campaigns of World War II did not impress most Americans in quite the same way as the World War I posters did. When we think of the posters of the forties, we are more inclined to remember the advertising posters. A glance at advertising in general in those years shows quite clearly that greater talent followed commerce than donated time to the war effort.

Although the industry continued to produce non–war-related posters through 1945, selection of the "100 best" was suspended in 1943 and 1944, so it is not possible to obtain an accurate overview of either quantity or quality for the period. The *OAAA News* did report extensively on the various war poster and civilian mobilization efforts for these three years but one must rely on only the 1940 to 1942 *100 Best Posters* plus the Art Directors Club annuals for an idea of the design. Unfortunately, these two publications were printed only in black and white.

In 1942, the Outdoor Advertising Art Exhibit Committee made three special awards for those posters that, in the committee's judgment, represented the best or at least the most characteristic of war effort posters. A waving flag with a quote from President Roosevelt encouraging bond purchases designed by Carl Paulson was displayed on more than 16,000 billboards and, for many, was the most memorable of the World War II posters. The second poster, a public service poster of Standard Oil of New Jersey, urges the public to "Double Up," not drive alone, and save gas and rubber. John Vickery, the artist, used the airbrushed stylization characteristic of his posters of the previous decade. It is one of the simplest and most sophisticated of all the World War II American posters. The third, by Marshall Reid, depicts a jeep and crew bouncing along with their trailer while we are urged to "Keep 'em Rolling" (by buying defense bonds and stamps).

The U.S. Department of Agriculture commissioned this 1942 caricature by Ren Wicks of a Japanese military figure. It typifies all manner of official and unofficial American World War II posters.

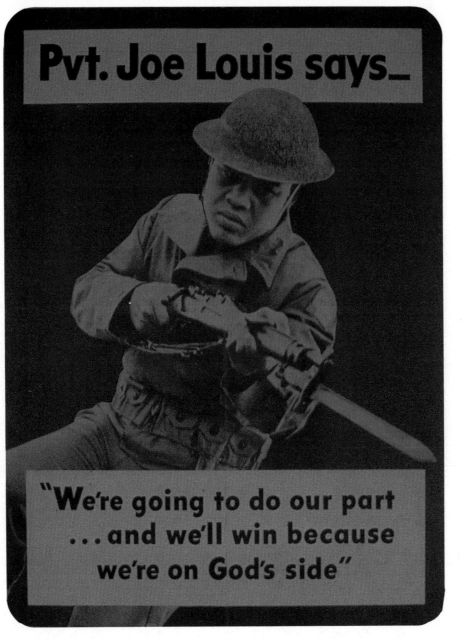

Pvt. Joe Louis says_

"We're going to do our part
... and we'll win because
we're on God's side"

This 1942 poster may have been the first of the few during World War II to feature a black American. It is notable for its portrayal of a black person who is neither a caricature nor a servant (51 x 36").

Right: The billboards in the War Effort Mobilization Campaign include, of course, a great many depictions of diving planes, enemy ships caught in the cross hairs of submarine telescopes, and brawny, perspiration-soaked men behind various types of guns. The creator of this melodramatic design, which reflects another creative approach, is unknown.

Among the 1942 posters servicemen appear for the first time in any quantity. But despite the sobering times, the general character of the advertisements, including those with vague or direct war effort themes, is anything but grim. Good humor and smiles prevail. Norman Rockwell's *Hop in Neighbor* for AMOCO is the best of the typical. AMOCO also released a conservation poster, *Make 'em last* by Joseph C. Leyendecker, in this same year. Lucian Bern-

hard, through the Joseph Katz agency, produced two strictly text posters for AMOCO suggesting that the viewer think, act, and work for victory and "not to wait but lubricate."

The 1942 Art Directors Medal was given to Jean Carlu for his *America's Answer! Production* (Office for Emergency Management), one of the great twentieth-century American posters. The Art Directors Club also chose posters by Vladimir Bobri, Joseph C. Leyendecker (a winner in the "cute humor" category), Norman Rockwell, Hayden Hayden, Walter Geoghegan, Lester Beall, and Joseph Binder. But Leonard Karsakov's *Prostitution spreads Syphilis and Gonorrhea*, despite its blame-the-woman approach, and Adolph Treidler's *Loose Talk Can Cause This* remain the strongest and graphically the most interesting of the Art Directors' selection after Carlu's *America's Answer! Production* poster.

In 1943, the Art Directors Club gave the Kerwin H. Fulton Medal to Douglass Crockwell for his *For Home and Country, Give* poster, a commission for the Community Chest. Ben Nason received the Award for Distinctive Merit for the *Boston* poster in his series for the New Haven Railroad; his *Nantucket* contribution was also cited. Other artists new to the competition were Alex Steinweiss (although his record sleeves for Columbia Records had been selected previously), Joseph Krush (to become well known as a children's book illustrator), and Erik Nitsche. Herbert R. Noxon, Walter Geoghegan, Adolph Treidler, and Edward F. Molyneux, frequently selected artists in earlier years, were still included.

Joseph Binder deservedly received the Art Directors Club Medal for his Sucrets series in 1944 and John A. Gaydos, the Award for Distinctive Merit for his threatening *Hands off the Americas* commissioned by the Office of the Coordinator of Inter-American Affairs. Harold von Schmidt, one-time Foster and Kleiser art director, but more widely known as a magazine illustrator and Western artist, received an award for distinctive merit for his *Give Us This Day* poster commissioned by the National War Fund. It is perhaps unkind to even mention the James Montgomery Flagg poster for WABC radio that the Art Directors Club selected. Surely it was chosen because of Flagg's name, not for the poster itself, which carries a somber likeness of singer Vera Lane.

Evidently the promise of peace released a great deal of energy in the Art Directors Club, for the 1945 exhibition was an ambitious

...MISSING IN ACTION...

SOMEBODY TALKED

V-HOMES ARE CAREFUL

THIS IS A V HOME

one indeed. In addition to the usual poster category, two additional categories were added, for the poster and other design commissions of the Office of War Information. George Lerner received the Kerwin H. Fulton Medal for a public service poster for Southern Pacific Company, *Main line to the Pacific War, Southern Pacific.* Howard Scott, Herbert Noxon, Harold von Schmidt, E. McKnight Kauffer, Joseph Binder, and Paul Rand all received attention for their designs for twenty-four-sheet posters.

Notable Office of War Information (domestic) twenty-four-sheet posters chosen were by Fred Ludekens, Garrett P. Orr, Otis Shepard, and Herbert Morton Stoops. George Giusti's series for the U.S. Department of Agriculture *Prevent Forest Fires* campaign remains to this day one of the few sophisticated series in this recurring national effort.

At war's end, the uncertainty of the future was as much on everyone's mind as the invigorating challenge of reconstructing the economy. Only the industrialists as a group seemed to be relatively free from anxiety. Artists and writers in general here and in Europe were anxious, to say the least. And so we went to the theater to see *The Iceman Cometh* (1946), *All My Sons* (1947), or *Death of a Salesman* (1949). Or, in 1946, we could watch William Wyler's *The Best Years of Our Lives* and Vittorio De Sica's *Shoeshine.*

Thank goodness for outdoor advertising's bright innocence. Here we could look at Haddon Sundblom's now famous *Yes* for Coca-Cola, Charles Towne's *Did somebody say Ballantine?,* Albert Dorne's *Now—Just Like Old Times!* (Heinz Ketchup), or Jon Whitcomb's *This is the Life* (Jantzen swimwear).

We had cars again in 1946 (after nearly four years), food, and travel, but not many memorable outdoor posters. There was optimism and good spirit but mainly pedestrian design. One series stands out: Muni Lieblein's posters for the U.S. Navy on how to drive a nail.

But most of us were much too busy consuming all the good things we were seeing on the billboards to be too concerned about anything else. Editorials in the *OAAA News,* articles in *Signs of the Times,* and the business press in general showed the way to substantial expansion of this medium despite the gains in radio advertising and that newest medium for advertising, television. Although commercially viable since the 1930s, it was not until the postwar period that refinements and mass production made TV sufficiently available to consider as a major advertising force.

In comparison with the explosion of vitality in periodical, packaging, and promotional design, twenty-four-sheet billboard design was much the same throughout the late 1940s. One poster in this period might be considered memorable, Kenneth W. Thompson's *Have a Coke* (1947) with its close-up snowscape unbroken except for a bottled Coke looking quite refreshing. The clients for single-sheet posters—public transit, the performing arts, and department stores—continued to attract the creative poster talent in those years. The New York Subways Advertising Company's campaign in 1948 was one such example, commissioning Jean Carlu, E. McKnight Kauffer, and others. This series of twelve posters was so popular that schools and universities in this country exhibited

them and exhibitions including them and the original art were hung in western Europe and in Japan.

Nonetheless, graphic design drawing on the influences already reaching us in the 1930s was rapidly confronting most reading Americans and certainly most Americans living in reasonably large cities. The work of Ben Shahn, Alexey Brodovitch, Leo Lionni, Hans Moller, Saul Bass, and Gene Federico, among numerous others, was widely seen and quite likely appreciated by the audience to which the outdoor industry was directed. Certainly many of the clients of outdoor advertising were or had used these same artists for other areas of design—why not for what they construed as their billboard audience? This question cannot be answered with any certainty at this distance, but we do notice that billboard styles remained cautiously static. Whether one is looking at late 1940s or early 1950s billboards, there is little change.

Several of Foster and Kleiser's artists—including Walter T. Warde, the company's general art director from 1940 to 1952—designed billboard structures as well as the billboards themselves. *Cool Off at the Beach* was typical of his early work.

Left: Joseph Binder's easily recognized airbrush style was in sharp contrast to the other styles represented in the billboard industry's mobilization series. It is regrettable that Binder was not responsible for the total design of the poster.

Overleaf, left: *Pepsi-Cola Hits the Spot* in a vintage forties billboard. Valentino Sarra and Harry Watts shared the photographic credits for this 1942 award winner; Edward F. Molyneux was the art director.

Overleaf, right: Haddon Sundblom greeted us in 1946 with this relatively timeless Coca-Cola poster. Sundblom received the first award in the billboard industry's competition that year.

Howard Scott's campaign poster for Wendell Willkie received an honorable mention in the 1940 Best Posters competition, but it failed to bring the candidate victory.

NO THIRD

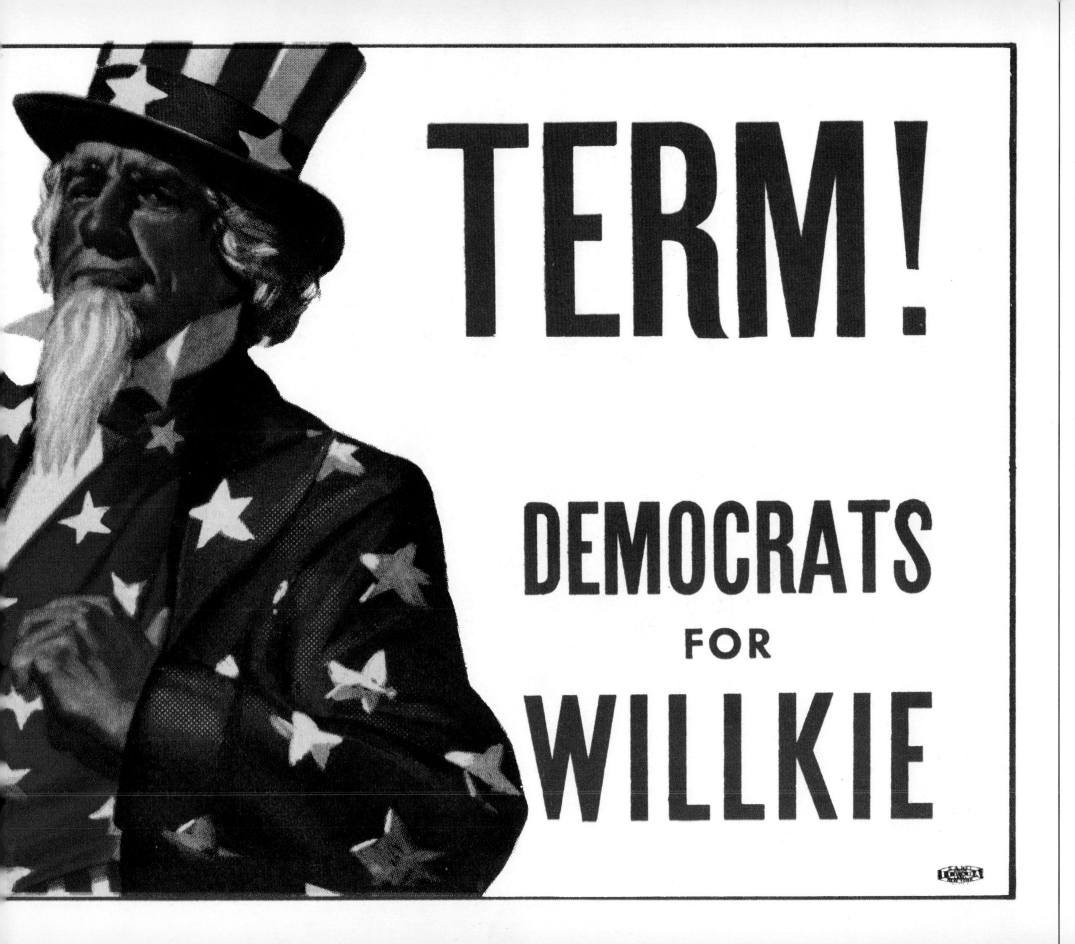

NEW CONTENT, NEW STRUCTURES, OLD CHALLENGES

Certain characteristics of decades stick in our minds. Some say the fifties were conservative, repressive years. Others recall the decade as a time of restoration of the family; certainly the beginning of the decade was marked by servicemen and -women returning and marrying. Families disrupted by the war were intent on a new beginning. Many manufacturers recognized this quite natural, species-protective phenomenon and moved to satisfy the increasing family-oriented needs with products to eat, drink, wear, and drive.

Looking at the outdoor advertising of the late 1940s and the early 1950s, one readily sees a continuity in theme, style, and idiom geared toward motivating Americans to buy and persuading those already motivated to keep on buying. The advertising is reassuring, as good advertising should be. Again, there are few hints of the problems of the time. Men are as much in charge as ever, even when stretched out on a chair or in a hammock. Women (and girls) are by turn coy or motherly, depending on what is being promoted. Children still look innocent. One good example is J. W. Wilkinson's *Quiet as a '50 Ford* (which won the Grand Medal Award of the Outdoor Advertising Association in 1950), in which a blond child lies asleep holding his stuffed panda. Wilkinson's agency and client well knew that an audience that perceives all is well (despite daily news reports) will be more inclined to buy.

And assurance in those early years of the 1950s was certainly needed by the mass of Americans who were, in varying degrees, alarmed by domestic and foreign events. In 1950 alone, Senator Joseph McCarthy was denouncing the State Department as harboring Communists; North Korea invaded South Korea and captured Seoul; China invaded Tibet; and Klaus Fuchs was passing British atomic secrets to Moscow. The next year did not bring any notable signs that life, in general, was going to be much easier than it had been a decade earlier. We were enmeshed in a war in Korea. The Rosenbergs were sentenced to death for spying against the United States. Worst of all, the Soviet Union successfully tested an atomic bomb.

Advertising—indoors and out—soothed us and reassured us, as we drove to and from work, that despite the wrongs "out there" American tables would be filled with plenty, our automobiles were the best, and our families were strong and contented because of what we were able to provide for them.

There were, as there always had been, public service billboards, but once again there were ominous messages among them, such as: *What Happened to that Pint of Blood You Were Going to Give?* (1951) and Garrett Orr's posters encouraging us to buy U.S. Defense Bonds to "Stem the Tide" and have the bonds rather than "Bondage."

However, the economy was growing, and billboard companies had their technical creative departments working overtime to dazzle us with mechanical and electrical innovations to heighten interest in the products displayed or, with improved lighting, give us a better chance to read them at night. One such improvement for night viewing was the adaptation of 3M's Scotchlite, a reflective substance initially developed for roadway signage in the 1930s, first used in outdoor advertising in 1947.

4 bedrooms, 3 baths... 2 FORDS

BONDS NOT BONDAGE

buy U.S. DEFENSE BONDS

Some of the more complex innovations of the period have come and gone. One, the "black light" painted display, in which fluorescent and phosphorescent paint combined with ultraviolet or mercury lighting, gave what the industry felt was an attractive "surprise element" when viewed at night. Mercifully for the hapless painters who had to paint these boards, this innovation was discontinued almost as quickly as it came: "black light" boards appeared in the 1950 outdoor industry's poster competition for the first time, and by 1952 they had been dropped. ("Bluelight," an innovative successor, is still being used, but only occasionally, and with limited success. This method of reflection relies upon a modification in the ink used to print the poster.) Mechanical devices animating painted displays or even paper posters—which got their start in the fifties—continue to be used in the nineties, mainly for local campaigns.

Yet the cutout image extending above the billboard itself was the most far-reaching innovation in the 1950s. Product or figure

cutouts above the painted board had been in use since the turn of the century. The Newark Billposting Company created a forty-foot-high Santa for the Hahne Department Store on Broad Street in Newark in time for the 1901 Christmas season. This promotional idea was tied to an army of eleven-foot Santas (same face and dress) on the major roadways leading into Newark and, the client hoped, to his department store. O. J. Gude in New York City had created cutouts for both board and side-of-building displays for a number of years spanning the turn of the century. Their cutout of a man's head extending above a wall painting for Wilson High Ball at the site of the old Sturtevant House (Broadway between 28th and 29th streets) was a landmark for years after its erection in 1904. On the other side of the continent, Varney and Green in San Francisco made elaborate cutouts for their clients from early in the century. The eagle in an ornamental "A" cutout for a Budweiser painted bulletin in 1904 has continued to be used by Anheuser Busch in painted and electrical displays throughout the country. These are but three examples of such work by major outdoor companies in the early years, when local carpenters were also being commissioned to create signage for on-premise advertising.

But the improved strength of the structures supporting the boards and the new variety of durable, synthetic materials allowed this style of display to flourish in the 1950s; it continues today. Cutouts and large painted bulletins (panels of paper-covered plywood) in which products and people were given unusual scale and proportion diminished somewhat the framed picture style that had been the convention of outdoor advertising for half a century. Yet the frame, while confining in one sense, actually emphasized the image cutouts. These extensions, in breaking the frame, developed into the "full bleed" board, without a frame at all. Within the decade, this led to experimentation with a segmented billboard of twelve four-foot panels, making what became a standard 14 x 48' bleed-face format, which allowed for custom cutout extensions. Thanks to this single development, panels could also be rotated from site to site in a city or region with the assistance of a boom truck. This breakthrough not only permitted most boards to be painted in the controlled environment of the studio (thus reducing costs and improving quality), but the advertiser was also assured a wider viewing of any given campaign. The industry had come a

long way from its initial search for the perfect structure and painting practice, which had begun nearly a century earlier.

Separating the billboard from other forms of advertising (to say nothing of other posters) and selling it as an identifiably distinct medium had long been a primary objective of the industry. By 1900, the first steps toward standardized structures had been achieved. But the search for the perfect structure, dignified yet relatively unobtrusive, has been a concern continuing to this day.

The industry debated and designed structures with increasingly frenzied creativity throughout the first five decades of this century. Two of the more interesting frames appeared in the wake of recovery from World War I: the "pilaster" and the green "lattice border" frame. Both achievements can be tied to the general retreat into fussy architectural styles allowed by the expanding economy of the 1920s. The pilaster frame added a bit of style, and green lattices surrounding the boards permitted a "blending with the verdant background." The pilasters, the sides of the frames in the form of buxom classical goddesses, had an appeal limited mainly to the West Coast, where they originated. These "lizzies," as they were irreverently called in the trade, were "designed to upgrade the neighborhood" and be a source of community pride with their attendant and requisite landscaping. But high costs and changing community taste ultimately doomed both of these frames: "lizzies" enjoyed only a short life (1923–31), and lattices survived only into the forties.

During the mid-1920s, one West Coast firm, Foster and Kleiser, maintained forty horticulturists on its payroll to select, design, and supervise the maintenance of the formal garden spots at the base of the rather spectacular pilasters. An offshoot of this particular effort was Foster and Kleiser's "Garden Clubs of the Air," which broadcasted gardening tips every Sunday morning for a number of years. Listeners were invited to come regularly to admire the gardens in front of the billboards in their towns and see the experts at work cultivating the flowers and lawns. The crash of 1929 brought hard times to the pilaster and garden programs, and by 1931, when the maintenance program was discontinued, most of the gardens had been transformed into easily maintained lawns. The frames were replaced with simpler structures that foreshadowed the developments of the next three decades.

An aerodynamic structure was next. The outdoor advertising event of 1946 was the streamlined design submitted to a committee of industry leaders (including Kerwin Fulton and George Kleiser) by Raymond Loewy—the foremost American industrial designer of this century, who gave us such varied designs as the Sears Coldspot refrigerator (1934), the shopping basket (for Lucky Stores, 1945), and the most memorable Studebaker models (1947 and 1953). With this new structure, the site once again received attention (in towns and cities at least). A simple apron of lawn contrasting with the white curved structure was considered to be the ultimate aesthetic achievement in the field and, in the main, was reflective of the industrial design concerns of the immediate postwar period.

Painted displays with and without cutouts became a permanent part of the annual outdoor advertising competitions in 1951. An unfortunate (by any standard) attempt to combine an early-twentieth-century architectural element from Chicago's Marshall Field department store with a Loewy streamlined lighted panel was awarded first place in the "embellished painted display" category that year. From that time and place to the Sunset Strip of the 1990s, the cutout design on a painted bulletin has developed from a rather clumsy and often unsophisticated attempt at attention getting to a riveting, slick presentation that is emulated the world over.

Painted displays or bulletins had become such an important element in outdoor advertising in the early 1950s that by 1955 the Outdoor Advertising Association established a Painted Display Department to coordinate services to the growing number of users of this form and plan annual "painted display" conferences. This department's officers also developed two new structures for painted displays, one for urban areas and one for highways. The size of the painted displays also grew in the 1950s and became standardized by the end of the decade at 14 x 48'.

Three-dimensional effects became possible through the in-

Saul Bass' 1950s film posters stood out from the mass, and this one is no exception. Reproduced in graphic-design annuals and journals and the subject of much commentary, Bass' work for Otto Preminger's *The Man With the Golden Arm* remains one of the great twentieth-century film posters.

Only convertible that outsells **FORD**

Scott Johnston, a graduate of the Art Institute of Chicago, was commissioned by J. Walter Thompson to announce Ford's 1953 convertible model.

creasing use of various types of plastic materials, but this addition to a bulletin was expensive. More often than not, it was provided locally as a one-of-a-kind design until a breakthrough at the close of the 1950s, when Simoniz developed a polystyrene form in the shape of a can of car wax. Such a plastic cutout, forty inches tall and nearly sixty inches wide, could be mass-produced and thus used economically on a national scale. This form was first used to promote a new car wax, Vista, in the spring of 1959. Its popularity continued into the 1960s, when other design techniques gradually replaced it.

The dominant design trend in billboards during the 1950s was the growing use of photography. In 1950, four of the *100 Best* billboards chosen included photographic components. By 1958, not only was a silver medal awarded to Bernard Gray for his Jax Beer design, a photo composition, but twenty-three other posters using photographic elements or complete photographs were also chosen. By the second half of the decade, billboards had attracted such accomplished photographers as Richard Avedon (Pabst, 1957; Schweppes, 1958), Irving Penn (Ancient Age, 1957; Lucky Strike, 1958), Valentino Sarra (7-Up, 1958), and Tana Hoban (Sealtest, 1958). All of these photographers continued working on billboards into the 1960s, when they were joined briefly by Herbert Matter (Morton Salt, 1960), Cecil Beaton (Modess, 1960), Garry Winogrand (Eastern Airlines, 1963), and others. Atlantic-Refining had used color photography for a number of years, featuring dramatic (as well as commonplace) American scenery as a backdrop for a traveling automobile presumably powered with Atlantic gas.

Starting in the late 1940s and continuing into the 1950s, there was some noticeable lessening of resistance among outdoor art directors and clients toward what continued to be called the "Euro-

Let Him Skip His BATH Tonight

A Public Service for

LITTLE BOYS

By Naegele Out door Advertising

NAEGELE

You can blow your head off—

it's

KLEENEX TISSUES

Soft! Strong! Pops up!

Above: An imaginative 1955 public service billboard addressing a local water shortage.

Below: Marge (Marjorie Henderson Buell), the creator of "Little Lulu," designed this odd cartoon illustration in 1950.

Right: Milton Greene created this 1953 eye-catching billboard for *LIFE* Magazine.

Overleaf, left: By the late fifties, the Jantzen diving girl, a billboard perennial, was sporting a strapless suit.

Overleaf, right: In addition to this 1955 design, Roy Spreter also created the award-winning *I Always Settle for Ritz* in 1951.

pean style" or stylized poster design. A 1951 example of this change could be seen in Paul Rand's Bab-O poster for the B. T. Babbitt Company. Another example, from 1954, was *Life* magazine's agency, Young and Rubicam, bringing the well-known French poster maker Raymond Savignac into a major campaign for *Life*. Savignac's first design for the series received the industry's First Grand Award that year. But other than John Vickery's *Don't Stall When it Says Go!* for Esso that same year, three other Savignac posters (for *Life*), and Otis Shepard's perennial airbrush designs for Wrigley, there is little else to comprise a stylized design trend. And despite the move toward photographic representation, most non-photographic billboards of the 1950s are heavy with painted real-

ism, full of unsophisticated humor (even for the time) and stereotypical images of smiling moms, dads, children, and pets.

Saul Bass provided welcome relief in mid-decade. In 1955, he received the Art Directors Club Medal for his thirty-sheet film poster for Otto Preminger's *Carmen Jones*. Bass also produced a number of noteworthy billboard-size film posters in this decade but did not receive any award attention by the outdoor industry. Sharing attention in the 1955 show with Bass, Roy Spreter (pert babies), Jack Welch (great babies and Tom Sawyer—type boys), and Dr. Seuss (of *Quick, Henry the Flit* and children's book fame), was Savignac once again with more posters for *Life*. The section on posters in the 1955 Art Directors Club annual was designed by Ladislav Sutnar, one of the great twentieth-century graphic designers to flee to this country (from Czechoslovakia) as a result of Nazi aggression. But none of his single-sheet posters were chosen for awards during the decade and only one billboard design idea by Sutnar is known.

At this time, a little-known collective of graphic designers and artists had been in business for about a year, working under the name of Push Pin Studios. The three principals, Milton Glaser, Seymour Chwast, and Edward Sorel, were to become so influential in a relatively short time that by 1970 the Louvre made the hitherto-unheard-of gesture of mounting a retrospective exhibition for a graphic design studio—and an American one at that. Though outdoor advertising's clients managed to keep a safe distance from the studio, art directors couldn't ignore them. From 1954 to the present, there have been few major American graphic design competitions or exhibitions that have not recognized one or more of the original team. By the close of the 1960s, Glaser and Chwast were known worldwide and had such a profound influence on poster making that there were few countries with a poster culture where their names were not known. The journal of their studio, *The Push Pin Graphic* (1956–81), was certainly a factor in their influence. Regrettably, few billboard-size posters have been produced by either. Chwast's outdoor series and single-sheet transit posters for *Forbes Magazine* are the exception.

By mid-decade, billboard design did become a bit leaner and the text, increasingly terse. But twenty-four- and thirty-sheet posters (the thirty-sheet poster became standard in mid-decade) of any

lasting design interest were primarily those selected by the Art Directors Club or included in *The International Poster Annual*, begun in 1949 by poster artist Walter Allner.

Saul Bass and Ettore Firenze produced a memorable poster for Pabco Paint in 1956 and Ludwig Bemelmans received the Award for Distinctive Merit in the same year for his illustration for the *You Get More in the New York Times* series. Walter Allner also produced a number of important billboard-size posters during this and the following decade.

A campaign for Safeway Stores that was to establish a graphic style for Safeway for years to come was Jerry Wright and W. J. MacDonald's (of J. Walter Thompson) effortless and clean grocery-list typography balanced by renderings of fresh fruits and vegetables. The campaign began in 1955.

The one exceptional year for billboards and, deservedly, for Saul Bass was 1957: Bass designed another Pabco Paint advertisement, art directed and designed a film poster for MGM's *Edge of the City*, and received the Kerwin H. Fulton Medal for another film poster, *Storm Center* (with Bette Davis). Two of Raymond Savignac's posters were selected (both for Procter & Gamble's Blue Cheer).

Though the poster design of the fifties seemed to merge right into that of the sixties, one decided change from the beginning of one decade to the other is the individual to whom awards were given. In the fifties, it was the artist, but in 1960 the *Outdoor Annual* gave the attention to the art director—a portent of what was to come. In 1971, credits to artists and photographers were dropped entirely from the annual outdoor advertising competitions for nearly a decade; they returned in the 1980s. This change is indicative of the direction of the creative process for billboards for the next twenty years.

For single-sheet posters, however, it was quite another matter. By the close of the 1960s, the single-sheet poster was experiencing an unprecedented renaissance. The anti–Vietnam War movement, the rock music rage, and various cultural movements that relied on the poster to promote their various causes contributed to this development. The poster art of this overall graphic phenomenon had its own effect upon the billboard, as can be seen in a few of the illustrations in the next chapter.

Worrying economic and government issues beset the industry in the late 1950s, not the least of which was the Federal Interstate Highway Act of 1954. In addition to its primary purpose of authorizing an expanded national network of highways, it greatly restricted the siting of billboards. This restriction had an immediate effect by diverting much of the industry's efforts away from expansion and into lobbying at every level of government. Not that the outdoor industry was suddenly determined to erect billboards along America's contemplated interstate highway system: the industry's half-century of concern for community and scenic interests was well known and documented. But it was concerned about the existing, standardized, member-owned structures along feeder roads and adjacent to the planned interstate highways.

With the controversy during the sixties, preceding the passage of the Highway Beautification Act of 1965, even more energies and funds would be diverted to lobbying, although "public education" is a more apt description. Explaining the distinction between on-premise signage created by a local sign shop, and carefully and systematically maintained billboards seemed to be a permanent challenge; at this late date, after some seventy years of concerted education programs, the industry continues to face it.

Another economically motivated change in the 1950s was the increasing use of the services of silk-screen companies such as Vandsco (now Vincent Printing Company, Chattanooga) and others to design and print billboards; most of their work was for local campaigns, frequently relying on stock design and typography, the outdoor equivalent of clip-art. One of the earliest major silk-screen companies producing stock posters was Thomson-Symon (founded in 1925), which by 1940 had offices across the country. Kubin-Nicholson of Milwaukee was another house of some size in those years, still very much alive. Today, these are joined by United Graphics (Lexington, Kentucky), Allentown Graphics (Allentown, Pennsylvania), and Independent (Hannibal, Missouri). But Vincent is probably the largest such plant under one roof: it prints and ships between forty and fifty tons of poster paper each month—the equivalent of 10,000–12,000 thirty-sheet billboards.

Despite the economic concerns in the second half of the fifties, a creative revolution was beginning to take place that would change forever the character of American advertising and, with it, the look of the billboard.

Raymond Savignac, a self-taught painter, graphic artist, and poster maker, created this 1956 prizewinner for Procter & Gamble.

Overleaf: In the late fifties, the billboard went gigantic, and its shape became irregular, as these ads attest.

Birds Eye, a subsidiary of General Foods, introduced Kool-Aid with John Howard's poster, a prizewinner in 1954. General Foods was aiming at a market of children and adolescents—thus the emphasis on price and convenience.

Left: When accepting an award for this billboard in 1955, Lifesavers' advertising manager stated: "Above all, we don't like long-winded selling messages."

Overleaf, left: Herbert Bayer's 1951 billboard for the Container Corporation of America came some fifteen years after Bayer had first begun working for the legendary Walter Paepcke, the corporation's president. It was the equally legendary N. W. Ayer art director Charles T. Coiner who had introduced Bayer to Paepcke. Paepcke, Coiner, and Bayer went on, collectively and individually, to influence American graphic design profoundly in the middle of the century.

Overleaf, right: Ken-L-Ration benefited from a light touch, as this 1955 award winner demonstrates.

Artist Jack Welch created this award-winning illustration in 1950 to introduce General Foods' Birds Eye frozen foods.

THE CREATIVE ENERGY OF THE SIXTIES

or advertising in general and outdoor advertising in particular, the sixties, seventies, and eighties began in 1959. And much of the past was not even prologue of what was to come. What happened in 1959 was a creative phenomenon quite different from what had gone before. It was fostered by what was at that time a surprising organizational concept for an advertising agency: merging copywriting and art direction into one "creative department." It sounded easy. To make it work it needed only the right combination of talent and the right leadership.

In 1959, when Karl Hahn, managing director of Volkswagen's North American marketing, approached William Bernbach of Doyle Dane Bernbach (DDB) to develop an advertising concept for his peculiar little ego-hampering car, even Bernbach himself could not have foreseen the long-term effects of his meeting Hahn's challenge. Aside from selling an unprecedented number of cars, Bernbach's response sparked a revolution that in time worked its way into those imperial preserves of American advertising, the venerable agencies whose names had been bywords for all that had been good and effective as far back as most advertising executives could remember.

What Doyle Dane Bernbach's Helmut Krone (art director) and Julian Koenig (copywriter) managed to develop in that critical year was simply an extended application of the principle that had already set apart the firm's campaigns for Ohrbach's, Levy's Jewish Rye, El Al, and Polaroid from all other advertising for similar products or services. The credo was: "Simplify . . . dramatize . . . make

crystal clear and memorable the message of the advertisement."

The Volkswagen campaign was a national test in many readily apparent ways, from name to style. This creative team not only passed the test but made that unlikely "peoples' car" the most readily identifiable automobile on the American highway for twenty years. DDB's advertising—indoors and out—did it (along with some help from quality control managers in Wolfsburg). And while in the process of giving masses of Americans a taste for practical foreign cars, William Bernbach and his increasingly talked-about team was changing forever what Daniel Boorstin described as "one of the most characteristic and most vigorous of American institutions": advertising.

The foundation of Bernbach's revolution was the concept that "advertising is fundamentally persuasion and persuasion happens to be not a science, but an art." Part of Bernbach's genius was his ability to spot creative people, draw them to DDB, and then inspire them to turn previously held views and practices about advertising upside down. They succeeded in the art of persuasion as no American advertising had before and maybe since.

Still, the old order didn't exactly give way overnight, but it persisted throughout the sixties, as it watched the unrivaled success of DDB (moving from $25 million in billings annually at the beginning of the decade to $270 million annually by 1969). Such major firms as Batten, Barten, Durstine and Osborn (BBDO), McCann-Erickson, J. Walter Thompson, and Young and Rubicam—all seasoned in outdoor advertising—observed and adjusted. Small firms where big decisions (and change) could take place quickly moved

COPPERTONE
Fastest tan under the sun!
—with maximum sunburn protection!
DON'T BE A PALEFACE
FOSTER and KLEISER

Small wonder

Cheap new.   Expensive used.

Mass transit.

Relieves gas pains.

You can afford to be choosy.

How to save up for a Porsche.

away from the traditional organization toward the creative team approach within a short time after their principals finished reading the latest DDB success stories in *Advertising Age*. Change was further spread throughout the sixties and well into the seventies as DDB associates left to start their own firms or join others.

The men and women of outdoor advertising responded enthusiastically to the new look being brought about by these changes. The Bernbach philosophy and the basis on which the creative revolution functioned was simply the bringing of "dead facts to life and making them memorable"—in a few seconds and at high speed, in

This thirty-sheet Schultz advertisement received an award in the 1960 annual billboard competition in Chicago. The campaign had successful TV exposure as well, featuring talking beer mugs.

"The same to you, Schultz!"

Right: In another example of the complementary nature of television and billboards, Lay's potato chips used the TV personality Bert Lahr in this 1967 poster campaign. In comic fashion, Lahr assumed various personalities on various boards. Lahr has been quoted as saying, "Those boards made me famous."

the case of billboards. That is what outdoor advertising had always been about. If the public was responding to direct, more cerebral advertising—and it obviously was—what advertising medium would dare hold back?

Billboards were also seeing increased competition from color television advertising. Television had another impact: it radically changed Americans' attention span. Practitioners of the new advertising responded to this by applying their principles to TV, often making the advertisements more interesting than the programs that carried them.

Simplified design, reduced and memorable text, and arresting wit were especially necessary in outdoor advertising. Americans were driving faster cars on wider streets and highways. The focused concepts of the new advertising as exemplified in the Volkswagen and Avis campaigns (DDB), the before-and-after ads of Papert, Koenig and Company for Coty, Naugahyde, and others, or what Stephen Frankfurt's leadership at Young and Rubicam did with their campaigns for Eastern Airlines or Lay's Potato Chips made the fantasy approach of earlier advertising—and thus much of the former billboard style—increasingly irrelevant.

With the focus on the creative team, with the art director and copywriter now on center stage, the artist and even the photographer needed to take a step back, as can readily be seen in the credits in the outdoor poster competitions from the 1960s on.

While the tumult in American advertising was being played out, with its direct and indirect effects on the billboard industry, American society was beginning to change its course as well. By the middle of the sixties change was manifesting itself not only in various basic areas such as family life, but even more fundamentally, in the way Americans of differing cultural and ethnic backgrounds began to perceive each other. The meaning of the Supreme Court decision of 1954 on racial segregation in public schools and the 1957 Civil Rights Bill protecting voting rights for blacks was slowly working its way into the thinking of white Americans. One of the most obvious visible examples of this was in the billboard. By the late 1950s, black Americans no longer appeared in stereotypical roles on billboards. World War II had effected some of this change, despite the fact that fighting groups were segregated throughout the war. An early (1942) example of nonstereotyped depiction of black Americans in posters was in a single-sheet recruitment poster for the U.S. Office of Facts and Figures. Private Joe Louis appears in a photograph with the message: "We're going to do our part . . . and we'll win because we're on God's side." Another poster in the following year was the War Production Board's *Twice a Patriot! Ex-private Obie Bartlett lost left arm—Pearl Harbor—Released: Dec. 1941—Now at work welding in a West Coast shipyard*. And there were others.

Unfortunately, in the late 1940s and into the 1950s, advertisers (and ad agencies) fell back to the prewar practice of presenting Cau-

128

FALCON

Minimalism shows its effect
on the billboard in this 1962 ad
for the Ford Falcon.

Left: The "Smart Women" campaign was
created during the late 1950s when tract
housing developments were being built
throughout southern California and utility
companies were vying with each other to
supply power. It ran until 1972.

casians as the dominant figures with blacks in a serving capacity. This practice continued, though infrequently, until 1956, when the last Aunt Jemima appeared on a billboard with her pancakes. Walker's Deluxe (Foote, Cone and Belding) used a black servant on a billboard for the last time in 1953. When the butler with a Walker's Deluxe bottle on his tray reappeared, he had become a Jeeves type, drawn by Ludwig Bemelmans.

Advertisers and agencies took a decade-long break before blacks began appearing again on billboards. By this time, in 1967, a transformation had taken place. In that year, the Detroit Police Department retained Campbell-Ewald for a promotion campaign to recruit policemen using a poster with the text: "There are never enough big men to go around." A dignified and serious-looking black officer in uniform was the department's model. The poster won the first award given by the outdoor advertising industry in the public service category in that year. By the early 1970s, black Americans were routinely portrayed positively, often with black and white together as equals. One example, a Stroh's Beer poster of black and white men drinking together (Doyle Dane Bernbach), set a new tone in 1970. In 1971, the Milk Foundation of the Twin Cities thought that its viewers were ready for an image of a black baby holding a bottle to a white baby in its *Everybody Needs Milk* campaign (Campbell Mithun Agency).

Through the post–World War II decades, Native Americans were no more visible than previously; their appearance was limited mainly to the Santa Fe Railway's stylized chief in headdress. By 1961, the railway had moved away from this image. A positive and poignant reappearance in the late seventies was the Morongo Company's public service painted bulletin *First Come, Last Served* with a sad but dignified chieftain against a starkly symbolic crimson background. Asians (Chinese, at least) appear infrequently, but invariably as wise men; they are no more offensively portrayed than wise, grandfatherly Caucasians.

The billboard industry received a boon in the 1960s from a quarter analysts had not predicted: major changes in attitudes toward the family meant that young people were marrying later. By the second half of the 1960s, it was clear that American societal values were shifting from the maintenance of the traditional nuclear family to values placing self above shared concerns or interests. Although divorce rates dropped briefly in 1954 and 1955, they began to rise into the final years of the sixties. The multiplication of households meant obvious new markets, if not overnight, then in less time than before.

The single-person household was a new consumer factor and demand for primary commodities (such as dishes, cooking utensils, and appliances) and services (the telephone) increased accord-

This "Best of Show" twenty-four-sheet poster was both designed and illustrated by Hal Riney.

Right: The Morton Salt girl has been trailing a stream of salt since 1911. The umbrella girl logo and the slogan "When it rains, it pours" were adopted for the company's packaging and advertising in 1914. The little girl received a hair, face, and dress makeover every decade, so she could stay abreast of the times. In 1965, Push Pin Studios designed this "Revolutionary Eggs" ad.

ingly. The leisure industry grew rapidly as the result of greater numbers of single individuals seeking recreation to fill the time formerly consumed in traditional family life. More and more young people with disposable income reoriented advertisers to the under-forty population.

The sixties also began to see the decline of mass-media general periodicals and the rise of highly successful special-audience publications. The increased quantity and quality of demographic and media research provided the means for an advertiser to identify its heavy users and select the medium, whether special-interest magazine, billboard, TV, or some creative combination that could cover the market most efficiently and effectively. Metromedia's Foster and Kleiser perceived this trend and commissioned a series of A. C. Nielsen studies in a number of its markets. These landmark studies enabled outdoor advertisers to define the extent of

their audience and the frequency of exposure to billboards on the basis of age, sex, and income. As audience segmenting became more and more a feature of marketing plans, outdoor advertising copy and placement reflected this trend.

The cognoscenti in the industry in the first years of the 1960s must surely have been pleased and amused as talk circulated about those odd paintings of larger-than-life objects, food, cars, and parts of cars that Leo Castelli, Martha Jackson, and other New York art dealers were showing to friends, collectors, and other dealers. Roy Lichtenstein, James Rosenquist, and Richard Hamilton (who may have started it all in 1956 with his "pop" collage) were far from household names. Pop art was not yet identified.

But it was apparent that the consumer society and the means for promoting consumption were in for a bit of visual criticism and parody when the group show "New Media—New Form," the first substantial exhibition of pop art in this country, opened in 1960 at the Martha Jackson Gallery.

And what did this phenomenon mean to the outdoor advertising industry and the look of the billboard, an acknowledged stimulus to the pop artists (and in the seventies to the super-realists)? A partial answer, read on two levels, is in a comment artist James Rosenquist gave to an interviewer at the Wallraf-Richartz Museum (Cologne) in December 1968: "I'm interested in the speed of recognition, of color in space, and the acceleration of nostalgia into the future." This sounded like a summary of what outdoor advertising leaders had been saying since the 1920s.

While there was a decided bent toward banality and selling by fantasy, all a stimulus to pop artists, the directness and humor of the creative revolution of the 1960s had all but conquered the banality and fantasy of the fifties and earlier. Billboards were beginning intentionally to blur the lines between advertising as we know it and graphic entertainment. And it still persuaded—now more than ever.

One need only look at what outdoor advertising did for food. Here, billboards convinced Americans in a relatively short time that food, served from a drive-in window, fast and simple, was better than all that fuss in the kitchen. Although restaurants serving a few entrees and serving them quickly had existed at least since Richard and Maurice McDonald lighted infrared lamps over a food

holding area in their San Bernardino hamburger restaurant in 1939, it was not until Ray Kroc came to the brothers with a franchise idea in 1954 that fast food for all who wished became possible.

This American food revolution, which dates from those years in the fifties, owes much to logos, billboards, on-premise signage and, of course, food; this was, indeed, a food-culture revolution in process. Doubters need only reflect on how many meals in any given week Americans eat at such franchised restaurants. What American child of three and older does not know the "golden arches," Colonel Sanders' face, Wendy's braids, the "word-burger" design of Burger King, or Frank and Dan Carney's Pizza Hut? For that matter, one might add the children (and adults) of Moscow, Tokyo, Paris, Berlin, and Oslo, among hundreds more cities. Fast-food chains are now entering a fourth decade using outdoor advertising to reinforce their presence by repeating their unmistakable logos while simultaneously promoting the classic American diet.

Pipe, chewing, and bulk tobacco (for cigarettes) had been advertised outdoors on the barns of rural America since the last decade of the nineteenth century. These painted barn walls were the most visible outdoor structures for tobacco ads for nearly half of this century; until the late 1980s, one could even make out the faint wording of Mail Pouch, Bull Durham, Prince Albert, and lesser-known brands in out-of-the-way places in midwestern and western states. One could only wish to see the expression on the barn painter's face of two generations ago watching today as a boom-truck crew hangs the last panel of the latest Marlboro painted bulletin on a single-pole structure somewhere in a southwestern landscape.

Tobacco, then and now, and particularly with the banning of its advertising on television in the early seventies, has been such an extensive user of billboards in every region of the country that it is difficult to imagine a growing shift away from this long-standing part of our culture.

In the 1960s, amusement parks and all manner of travel-related services increased and today continue giving us some of the more spectacular painted bulletins—e.g., cutouts of screaming children in the theme park's water-borne craft, planes extending from the top of signs, and larger-than-life hosts and hostesses inviting us to spend the night in their hotels.

The record industry's dramatic use of billboards along Sunset Strip in Los Angeles starting in the 1960s is famous throughout the world. But this highly charged contest of competing record companies drawing the public's attention to current stars and releases is only the latest example of their use of outdoor advertising.

With recording stars (full face and in profile), Marlboro men, and fast-food logos all high on the skyline at the close of the 1960s, what more could be added? Our national reserves for product and service inventiveness were only beginning to be tapped. The style

In 1962, Mars Candy used a simple, childlike illustration to promote its product.

and content of what was to come on billboards and how it would be designed and displayed was an open question, given the graphic exuberance at either end of the decade. It was likely to be, as implied in a comment by art director Alvin Eisenmen in a 1959 Type Directors Club seminar, "We seem to have a consistent natural variety."

That variety certainly characterized American graphics of the sixties. We began with Saul Bass, Will Burtin, Paul Rand, George Lois, and an equally talented score and ended with Peter Max, Victor Moscoso, and John Alcorn. A gross simplification—but fortunately for graphic design in the seventies and beyond, the legacy of the former group has outlived the latter.

Left: *New Yorker* cartoonist Henry Syverson's Yellow Pages ad for Pacific Telephone in 1965. Outdoor advertising is frequently compared to the classifieds, since it is an inexpensive means of reaching a large audience.

Few can resist a sandwich, which became a selling point for Holsum Bread. Holsum used extensions to add extra space to the standard 14 x 48' billboard structure (1965).

Right: This 1961 Sanka board is the first of the free-form bulletins of the 1960s. Free-forms took advantage of the extra footage provided by extensions to the basic 14 x 48' structure.

Overleaf, left: In 1969, Pan Am promoted its flights down under in a particularly graphic way.

Overleaf, right: As America moved into the sixties, diet, health, and fitness concerns increased. Cereal companies capitalized on this, as is clear in this 1962 ad for Grape Nuts.

Sydney.

As part of a series advertising packaged food, Kern's displayed this ad in January 1968. Industry experts agree that this campaign included some of the best illustrations ever displayed on a billboard.

Left: Using the painted billboard, Swanson introduced its name and the convenience of frozen dinners to Americans who were concerned with saving time. Produced in 1959, the ad was created to combat the general impression that frozen food was not tasty.

In 1966, this controversial billboard appeared on New Jersey highways leading into New York City.

Left: Richard Nixon won the 1968 presidential election by the narrowest of margins. This ad represents the sweeping thirty-sheet billboard campaign that reached the electorate for thirty days, including Election Day.

Overleaf: This unforgettable billboard was unveiled at the National Outdoor Advertising Convention in 1967, and within sixty days it was on display across the country. After receiving much media attention throughout the world, it was submitted in the first International Poster Show at the request of the organizing committee.

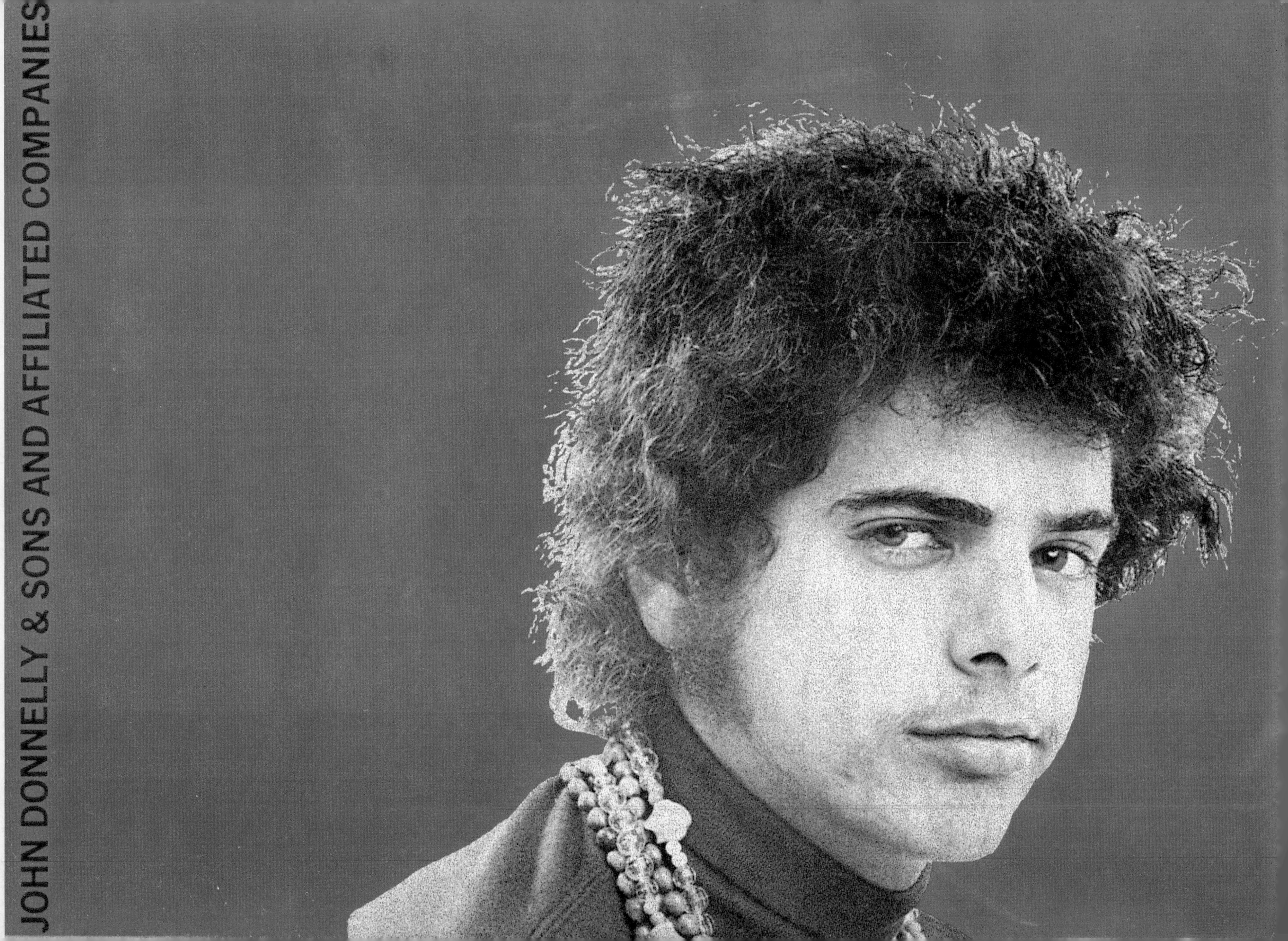
JOHN DONNELLY & SONS AND AFFILIATED COMPANIES

BEAUTIFY AMERICA

get a haircut

With the post-Cold-War popularity of secret agent James Bond and the 007 movie series, Jim Beam liquor appealed to a mass audience that enjoyed thrilling escapades. The bold illustrative style influenced by Peter Max is typical of the sixties.

Right: In reinforcing the public service message "To get a good job, get a good education," the Advertising Council and the U.S. Department of Labor petitioned their audience to seek escape from poverty.

Overleaf, left: The convenience appliances known as "white goods" freed housewives from certain chores. This 1968 ad combined sixties argot with simple layout. As these appliances supposedly gave women more free time, advertisers like Knoxville Utilities boomed.

Overleaf, right: For many years, 7-Up was bought mostly by older Americans. Then, in 1969, realizing its growth potential depended on gaining a younger market, the company began to sell its product as an alternative to cola—thus the "Un-Cola" campaign. Using billboards with the same illustration that was already appearing on record jackets and wall posters, 7-Up enjoyed a thirty percent increase in sales in the first year of this campaign.

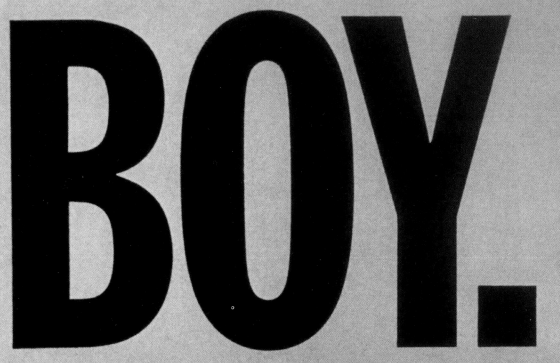

BOY.

Drop out of school now and that's what they'll call you all your working life.

To get a good job, get a good education.

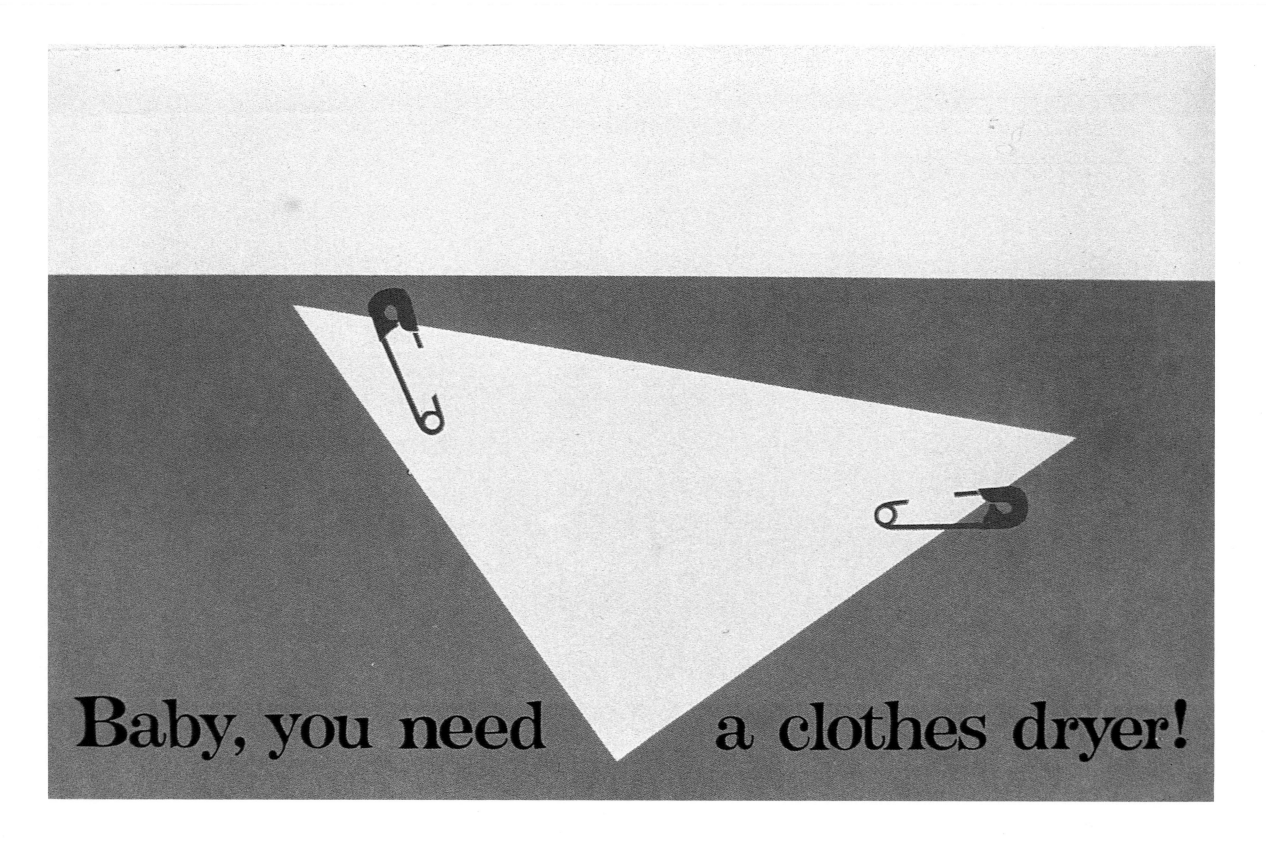

CREATIVITY, CONSERVATION, AND CONSCIENCE

Getting over the late 1960s took a while, but, by the mid-seventies, the social aberrations of those transition years did seem to self-correct for the mass of Americans. The steamy, Day-Glo graphic design that grew directly out of the amalgam of the drug and rock culture, the graphic style of the anti–Vietnam War movement, and social protest graphics in general were quickly committed to history, with only sporadic revival in the idiosyncratic borrowings of 1980s designers too young to remember much of that time.

But a second look at early seventies billboards, which featured graphics derived from what was going on in society around them, conveys the feeling that the designers were striving for an appearance of contemporaneity—but often achieved only a forced look.

Probably what moved us quickly away from that brief and somewhat chaotic era were the oil crises of 1973 and 1979. The first, at least, was an event that suddenly shook us into thinking about our national purposes and our individual goals. The energy crises showed us our vulnerability. Decisions half a world away could affect how often we would drive our cars and how fast; they made us reconsider the size of our cars and the temperature of our homes in winter. Bicycles and feet were rediscovered as modes of travel. Public transportation was temporarily revived as an alternative to having one rider per car.

But for sheer market impact, the seventies saw the reawakened interest in the remarkable design of our bodies, which brought dietary changes—new, healthier food—and a new level of concern for fitness. Health food, exercise equipment, weight-loss centers, and diet drinks not only for the middle-aged or overweight but for young people . . . all became substantial factors in the economy, and in billboards. The major soft drinks (Pepsi-Cola, Coca-Cola, 7-Up, Dr. Pepper) all rushed to billboards in this era with their new low-calorie drinks. On the other side of the health issue, the seventies also witnessed the first extensive use of outdoor advertising by hospitals and medical insurance companies. Even hospital emergency rooms promoted themselves to travelers. Understandably, most such health care advertising was local or regional.

Care for the soul was not excluded. From before World War I into the 1950s, churches had advertised, often with donated space. The public service posters encouraging worship were not only a consistent part of American outdoor advertising in these forty years but the outdoor industry house organs regularly featured local and regional religious advertising. In the sixties, such interest declined, but by the mid-seventies it had revived, focusing on a different audience—young people. The southeastern and southwestern states were especially known for such campaigns.

The most comprehensive national billboard undertaking of a religious nature at any time in American outdoor advertising history surely must have been that of Campus Crusade for Christ, a Los Angeles–based nondenominational student ministry. In 1976, this organization saturated 181 major metropolitan areas with its "I found it" teaser posters. The "tell" posters, which followed, gave telephone numbers; dial the number and you'd get an evangelical response. The organization reported in excess of a half-million "decisions for Christ."

Shirley Cothran

Miss America 1975

In 1975, the Institute of Outdoor Advertising developed a campaign to measure billboards' effectiveness. The concept featured Shirley Cothran, the newly crowned Miss America, on billboards that were displayed across the country. Her name recognition soared after this campaign, which was welcome news to the billboard industry.

The smile spoke directly to Colgate's cavity-free audience in 1989.

Another unusual mid-decade use of billboards was a market test of the medium's effectiveness. The Institute of Outdoor Advertising (IOA), the research arm of the industry, decided to use the 1975 Miss America contest as a test for recognition. Like all such events, it had considerable electronic and print media coverage at the time. Shortly after the pageant and the announcement that Shirley Cothran had won, a survey was taken which revealed that relatively few people in the sample could remember her name. The IOA then posted Cothran's photo on thirty-sheet billboards across the country. After the boards had been up for thirty days, interviewers again questioned Americans on her identity. The results were remarkable—awareness nationwide had increased nearly 940 percent! This was welcome, confirming news for the outdoor advertising industry and its users. It was impressive to potential advertisers, and, as expected, attracted many new clients such as cable TV, electronic equipment (from beepers to computers), and the waterbed.

The U.S. government, longtime outdoor advertiser in wartime and in peace with its public service campaigns—from forest fire prevention to energy conservation—now entered the field on an expanded scale with numerous posters for fuel conservation and military recruitment. Then there was the launching of Express Mail when efficient private overnight mail services began taking more and more of the post office's business.

Local government anticrime and "support-your-local-police" posters began appearing frequently in the seventies in nearly every major American city. Unfortunately, these campaigns were not always the most sophisticated in terms of design. By their very nature, they were not conducive to the humor we had begun to expect from the more creative campaigns of the 1960s.

Creativity, however, was readily found in product marketing, at its best in the soft drink field, especially in the 7-Up Un-Cola ads. The humor appealed to an age group somewhat jaded by *Harvard Lampoon*–style humor and was so effective that 7-Up sales soared to quite unexpected levels. One unintentional test of the popularity of this particular campaign was in 7-Up's reaction to a multitude of requests for posters: they offered to *sell* a reduced version of one of the billboards as a poster. Young people responded by sending in 48,000 checks and money orders.

It may just have been youthful rebellion—combined with the fuel crises—that brought the motorcycle back to American highways and tree-lined streets. But there are many who would hurry to credit the effective outdoor marketing of the affordable Japanese models. Even the most conservatively comfortable male physically capable of mounting this new breed of cycle likely flirted with the fantasy of riding one of the Hondas, Kawasakis, Yamahas, or Suzukis right off the boards. This competition undoubtedly helped sales of such domestic cycles as Harley-Davidson, which also returned to billboards in the seventies.

If any ever believed that outdoor advertising firms and their clients lost their conscience somewhere at the close of the 1960s (public service campaigns briefly declined in 1968 and 1969), a reassessment of the public service advertising in the seventies should cancel any such doubts. Certainly, the good side of the social revolution of the late sixties brought a greater awareness of social needs, inequality, environmental issues, and the like. The result was reflected not only in the advertisements mentioned previously, but in public utilities matching local, state, and national governments' concerns with saving water, heat, and fuel.

The 1976 American bicentennial celebration inspired successful tie-ins for everything from Levi's to automobiles, often with messages that were more history than product. In a nation not noted for historical reflection, many Americans, at least for a year, paused for a positive backward glance, courtesy of advertisers and public service agencies alike.

The bicentennial year brought outdoor advertisers and companies a moment of encouragement. Joining them were other Americans who had the opportunity to see urban signage and billboards with the perspective of a group of highly influential architects and designers. Robert Venturi, Denise Scott Brown, Steven Izenour, and George Rauch conceived the exhibition "Signs of Life: Symbols in the American City." Mounted at the Smithsonian's Renwick Gallery in Washington, D.C., it showed us how our signage and our outdoor advertising affect us for good—and bad. The pedagogical value of such an exhibition may merit having one once every decade.

The most important change for the outdoor advertising industry in the past twenty years, aside from the corporate restructuring

What could be fresher than Byerly's Corn?
After seeing this startlingly simple and
lifelike image, one might well wonder.

resulting from mergers and acquisitions, has been technical.

During the seventies, the growing use of computers in industry led a group of billboard companies to commission studies at the Massachusetts Institute of Technology in the painting of bulletins by computer. The quality of a national advertiser's design often varied from market to market, largely because of a shortage of skilled painters. There are few schools to train painters in this art; it is a skill most often acquired through apprenticeship on the job. Though not a substitute for hand painting, computer painting does provide speed; refinement will undoubtedly improve its quality.

The seventies could be viewed as a transition decade for outdoor advertising. Good things happened, but better things came with the eighties: more technological advances, highly successful product campaigns, improved graphics, research advances. Even diehard billboard adversaries could not help but admit that some designs were beginning to take the viewer's breath away. Those Naegele painted bulletins for Byerly's food and drink and the Nike boards are but two examples that have shown just how good outdoor advertising could be.

These and other virtually wordless (except for the product name) billboards raise interesting questions: is our society approaching "wordlessness"? Are we moving too quickly to read? Or are these boards examples of the ultimate billboard where there is only an object and a trade name? Are these boards actually contributing to the lessening of tension by giving us a brief reprieve from the lyrics on our radios? Is their verbal silence heightening the strength of the image by acting as counterpoint to the daily babble and wordiness of the other media, our neighbors, and our associates?

There is little question about the memorable campaigns of the eighties, whether the Gatorade bottles in the eyes of the athlete, the cyclist riding the red word "Honda," the Colgate toothpaste tube creating a smile, or that ultimate logo-into-satisfied-response of McDonald's, "M-m-m-m-m." All of these, and many others, rely on the message from the logo or product image to reinforce the manufacturer's or product's presence, rather than explain its importance or persuade us to buy.

The copywriters of the eighties continued the seemingly endless exploitation of the pun, a trend begun in the 1960s that shows

no sign of weakening, no sign of being overdone. Some puns, however, were intentionally directed to an adolescent audience—for example, the San Diego Zoo's highly successful and award-winning series with its play on the name or the most characteristic action of the animals depicted. One example depicted an orangutan mother with her offspring riding on her shoulder and the phrase "Double-Deck Bus Tours."

A few others worth mentioning and deserving of a second look: the Justin Boot Company's *Truth, Justin, and the American Way*; John Deere lawnmowers' *Looks Like Deere Season* captioning an overgrown lawn; *United Shines to Florida*; and *Miró, Miró, on the Wall* for the Minneapolis Institute of Arts. The unspoken rule came to be: six words or less.

Critics have complained that in the eighties outdoor advertising reflected the dominant political trend of lessening concern for social problems, and little concern for conservation, health problems, or the environment. On the contrary, crime- and drug-fighting posters appeared throughout urban and suburban areas throughout the eighties, just as before. The problems of AIDS, child abuse, and spouse abuse were new themes and very much present in the second half of the decade. The perennial fund campaigns—United Negro College Fund, United Way—were also there, along with the long-standing drives for supporting research into special diseases. And remember how the decade began in 1980 with billboards calling for release of the U.S. hostages in Iran?

A quick review of the eighties reveals several interesting first-time or stepped-up billboard users. The legacy of the oil crises and the move to smaller, more economical cars brought these new models to the billboard: Ford's Pinto and Escort, Chevrolet's Chevette and Citation, and the entire range of the foreign competition from Japan and Germany, and, at the end of the decade, Korea. Vegetable, fruit, dairy, and beef grower associations were suddenly much more aggressive in the 1980s in using outdoor advertising, as were candy and gum manufacturers. Such longtime billboard advertisers as Clark and Wrigley were joined by M&M's, Rocky Road, Big Hunk, and Bit-O-Honey.

The U.S. government continued to use billboards for recruiting and Express Mail, and in a quixotic effort to increase train use it produced posters promoting Amtrak.

Tiger River.

A new twist.

At the San Diego

MIRÓ MIRÓ ON THE WALL.

MINNEAPOLIS INSTITUTE OF ARTS

The Minneapolis Institute of Arts made one of its holdings do double duty as a billboard illustration in 1987.

The proliferation of car telephones stirred a number of advertisers with appropriate products or services to provide a phone number for orders or inquiries right on the billboard. Sufficient success has meant the continuation as well as expansion of this practice.

The one campaign of the 1980s that probably will linger in the most memories is what Chiat/Day did for Nike during the 1984 Olympics in Los Angeles. The painted bulletin of Carl Lewis leaping off the edge of the billboard into the sky epitomizes that campaign. Converse, not Nike, was the official Olympic shoe, but the Nike painted bulletins and walls captured the attention of not only the on-site spectators, but the multiplied millions who watched on television. Even the press noted with enthusiasm this quite amazing outdoor campaign by this highly successful agency founded by Jay Chiat and Guy Day in 1968.

California–based Chiat/Day demonstrated that an advertising agency in a city other than New York or Chicago could create advertising that would generate memorable sales and even contribute appreciably to world advertising folklore. Any agency that can take an even homelier car than a Volkswagen beetle—the first Honda to be unloaded in an American port—and establish it firmly in the American market, as Chiat/Day did, deserves a separate chapter on what can be done with billboards. The firm did this in the early 1970s while establishing an audience for zany television commercials that worked.

Another example of Chiat/Day's approach is its billboard campaign for Yamaha motorcycles. In 1977, when Chiat/Day was retained, the competitor, Honda, was showing a bike, a boy, and a girl under the headline "Follow the Leader" on boards all over Los Angeles. Jay Chiat immediately came up with the slogan "Don't follow anyone." When the Yamaha billboards—which showed only that text and a motorcycle in a mildly aggressive stance—were placed next to or a short distance behind the Honda boards throughout the county, the wished-for response was certainly forthcoming. Honda executives probably died a little each day as they drove to their offices reading these boards and being reminded of how much they had lost when they left Chiat/Day with their car account in 1974.

LOOKS LIKE DEERE SEASON

Nothing Runs Like a Deere

Chiat/Day (now Chiat/Day/Mojo, with offices in major cities) continued its success throughout the 1980s with its campaigns for Alaska Airlines, the Disney Channel, Porsche, California Cooler, Nynex, Reebok, Nissan, and many others.

Major changes in the billboard industry took place in the eighties, notably the acquisition in 1985 of the eighty-five-year-old Foster and Kleiser Company by Patrick Media Group. Gannett Company, Inc. acquired Combined Communications in 1979, and Eller Outdoor became part of Gannett Outdoor. Morris Communications acquired Naegele in 1985. But of greater importance, perhaps, than these mergers was the move to advanced technology in every area, from computerization of the internal management of day-to-day operations to the actual printing of posters. Some of these changes employed existing technology, but others grew out of technology that was developed or adapted to the outdoor advertising industry's specific needs.

At the same time, a plastic material was developed that provided a one-piece 14 x 48' surface on which to paint. This was a substitute for the four-foot plywood sections and presented a durable, seamless surface. The leading firms in developing a commercial computer painting technology were Metromedia Technologies and Computer Image Systems.

Meanwhile, Gannett Outdoor adopted a sleeker billboard structure called the Trim Panel. It was the first major modification of the Loewy streamlined panel of the forties, replacing the foot-wide Loewy frame with a narrow inch-and-a-half molding with curved corners. Its purpose was to lessen the distraction of the structure to the advertiser's copy and provide a more dramatic display of bleed-face posters. It was not a totally new concept, however—Donnelley had used a similar curved corner panel for more than eighty years and Foster and Kleiser had employed a similar panel called a "picture frame" in the 1950s. Nonetheless, the Trim Panel is considered by many industry leaders to be the panel of the future.

These revivals of past panel designs, variations on the materials for structures and boards, and advanced technology for printing the surface will likely give the billboard a decided advantage in the years to come.

FLY WITH ME.
UNIVERSAL STUDIOS. ORLANDO 1990.

FLY WITH ME.
UNIVERSAL STUDIOS. ORLANDO 1990.

A series of 1990 New York-area billboards advertising the Nynex Yellow Pages were simulated tear-outs. A number of them—in addition to the example here—relied on a visual pun: the "Stains" entry carried food stains, and "Marriage Broker" consisted of two torn pieces of paper waiting to be fitted together.

Left: In the late 1980s—after some time of little billboard use—the entertainment and tourism industries returned to the medium. Universal played to a wide audience with this 1990 ad for that popular alien E.T.

Overleaf: Public awareness of the issue of physical abuse to women was heightened by this strongly worded 1988 billboard (left). Another attempt to reach an audience of abused women (right) was aided by the concept's strong visual and emotional impact and the inclusion of a hotline number.

When Mr. Right Starts Throwing Lefts.

Cornerstone

Help For Battered Women.

NAEGELE
TWIN CITIES

Some women will never talk to anyone about being abused.

L.A. BATTERING HOTLINE (213) 392-8381

Mothers Against Drunk Driving (MADD) won an Obie award and a considerable amount of attention with this powerful statement showing the actual car that was in the crash.

Right: This image from 1970 was created for the Ad Council to heighten awareness of the effects of drug use. Its visual impact cannot be disputed, and its message is timeless.

Forest fires burn more than trees.

FOSTER and KLEISER

166

The Minnesota Zoo's tiger-clawed board from 1989 is a uniquely effective use of cutouts.

Left: Contributing its services to forest-fire prevention since 1942, Foote, Cone & Belding created this ad for the U.S. Forest Service and the Ad Council in 1987.

Overleaf: Although Converse was the official shoe of the 1984 Olympics, Nike advertisements captured the public's attention.

Truth, Justins and the American way.

Justin

The Justin Boot Company wittily utilized a Superman motif in this ad, which won a 1987 merit award in the Outdoor Advertising Association's annual competition.

Left: Bo knows billboards. Another unforgettable Nike image from 1984.

Above: Painted partially by hand and partially by computer, this unusual bulletin, which first appeared in 1988, represents a new technique in billboard design.

Below: In 1985, Benetton integrated racial differences into the company's attempt to speak to a wider and younger audience. The ad campaign, which eventually moved into other advertising media, started outdoors, aiming to create a high-fashion image.

Left: Calvin Klein jeans used strong fashion photography in what appears to be an effortless layout in 1982.

Overleaf, left: Reminiscent of its earlier ground-breaking campaign, Volkswagen's 1986 billboard for the GTI used little copy with exceptional photography. VW promoted this car as having the speed that the early Beetles lacked.

Overleaf, right: A Foster and Kleiser award-winning 1983 billboard for Honda, one of the decade's most memorable campaigns.

© 1983 AMERICAN HONDA MOTOR CO., INC.

FOSTER and KLEISER

CREATIVITY, CONSERVATION, AND CONSCIENCE

Above: Larger than life, realer than real, the top of a Bloody Mary beckoned on behalf of Kamchatka vodka in this 1987 billboard.

Below: For nearly a decade, Maker's Mark Liquor effectively communicated its message with a unique approach to product photography. With the emphasis placed on image—and no copy—this approach clearly separated the advertiser from the competition.

Right: Surf's up! This 1987 Obie winner graphically tied Anheuser-Busch's product to a carefree, active life-style.

And Nothing But The Moo.

California Fresh Eggs

Above: A 1986 California Milk Advisory Board campaign used wit and vivid illustration to allude to the naturalness of cheese.

Below: In 1987, when the California Egg Commission was faced with an inventory oversupply, it chose a campaign utilizing layouts that promoted the egg as being more than a breakfast staple. With creative photography and simple copy, the food became associated with a certain life-style. The demand became so great that the commission soon had a different kind of inventory problem and had to import eggs from out of state.

Left: This 1987 billboard for Kemps ice cream brought this relatively modest-size Minnesota company awards and a geometric increase in sales.

SURGEON GENERAL'S WARNING: PREGNANT WOMEN WHO SMOKE

patrick

The red tent has represented Marlboro cigarettes for twenty-five years. Although the Marlboro audience was originally thought to be female, a tough and rugged cowboy has long been the brand's signature. This painted bulletin is dated 1988.

182

One of the few billboards designed by Seymour Chwast also ran as a magazine cover in 1985.

Left: Metropolitan Life ran its first billboard campaign in 1987. The boards were located in twenty-one markets nationwide. Media planners felt that since many in their target audience (eighteen- to forty-nine-year-olds) had grown up with Snoopy, he and the other characters would make them feel comfortable. The designs have always used extensions and three-dimensional effects to attract attention.

Overleaf: All of the billboards in this 1989 Club Med campaign used highly stylized photography to create enticing dream-filled escapes for the upwardly mobile singles crowd.

CLUB MED
The antidote for civilization.™

EPILOGUE

When one comes to the conclusion of a compilation such as this and looks back at all that for one reason or another has had to be eliminated, one realizes that the history of an industry or an association cannot be one book, or even two. There are individual biographies of varying lengths to be written on the remarkable personalities who created outdoor advertising as an industry and who continue it to this day: the men from C. S. Houghteling to John Kluge with scores in between, including such as R. J. Gunning, Thomas Cusack, and O. J. Gude, who were active before the 1891 reorganization years. The list from 1891 to the present would certainly include Barney Link, Kerwin Fulton, the O'Mealia men, the Donnelleys (through nearly 150 years), John Paver, Alfred Van Beuren, Burr W. Robbins, George Kleiser, Walter Foster, Philip Tocker, John D. Walker, J. Q. A. Chapman, George A. Treyser, Edward Stahlbrodt, Charles F. Bryan, Thomas H. B. Varney, George L. Chennell, Leonard Dreyfuss, E. L. Ruddy, Samuel Pratt, W. W. Workman, Clarence U. Philley, W. Rex Bell, and Ted Turner. Additional contemporary giants of the industry include R. O. Naegele, Ross Barrett, Dean White, Hal Brown, Sr. and Hal Brown, Jr., Carl Eller, and Don Reynolds. Individuals providing key leadership during the past thirty years include Robert B. Lee, Charles Burkhart, Frank Hardie, Richard Condon, Barry Ackerly, Kevin Reilly, Sr., Jack Armstrong, Ray Vehue, Tom Norton, Harry Goss, Herman Green, Jim McLaughlin, Richard Estus, Eric Myhre, and James Roddey.

Then there is the story of the unsung heroines of the industry, women who took over companies when their husbands died of overwork or accident; they ran tight (often tighter) shops, judging from fragmentary accounts. A major book waits to be written on women billboard artists, as well as the female single-sheet poster artists whose work went unsigned. For every Blanche McManus or Florence Lundborg, there were dozens who dropped out of poster history without a footnote, only a signature on a poster. Some of the better-known figures such as Neysa McMein or Ethel Reed received attention in their time but were later forgotten. And then there were all those women designers whose work we know mainly from cover after cover of *The Poster*, the industry's journal.

Anyone looking at this book's index for names of poster designers—men or women—may wonder why a given name is not there. There are simply too many to include: from 1926 to 1960, the poster annual includes a roster of more than 2,000 artists. We know little or nothing about many of them.

Then there are the small companies that have come and stayed—such as Bay Advertising Company (Ashland, Michigan), in the Otis family since 1923 and operating under the same name since around 1891; the Maxwell Company, also operating for more than 100 years; and those countless firms that lasted but a few years or more, merged into larger companies, or went by the way, and whose names are not even remembered.

The technical history of the industry has, alas, been treated fleetingly in these pages. We have mentioned only a few structural design changes over the years, and there were many. We've passed over the electric sign and the combination of electric sign and billboard, for that subject deserves a major monograph of its own.

THE FUTURE

Undoubtedly some readers will have looked in vain for mention of one of the favorite outdoor advertising ventures of the century, the Burma Shave signs. Had they been billboards by our definition—not signboards—or had they been printed on paper—rather than painted on wood—we might have spent some time with them. But they, like other outdoor advertising campaigns that were not strictly billboards (such as broadsides) have had to be omitted.

In the last chapter, some attention was given to the new technology, but only in passing. From an aesthetic standpoint, it may be of interest to reiterate that design and technology in concert are improving the general physical appearance of billboards. Structural advances have allowed streamlined forms—such as the Trim Panel mentioned earlier—that blend better into the landscape. Using aircraft-grade alloys in structural supports has also allowed more creative siting; with the greater strength of these materials, billboard structures can withstand hurricane-force winds.

Computer advances have provided the industry with almost limitless opportunities and insured against its becoming obsolete for any technical reason. Computer-assisted painting already en-ables creative directors to assure consistent quality in the reproduction of artwork. It is anticipated that in the future designers will be able to create sales messages with a few strokes of an "electronic brush" and, by executing a series of computer commands, have the image appear on billboards throughout the country. The face of the future billboard may more closely resemble a television screen than the painted or papered surface of today, with the advantage of the possibility of changing the message as often as necessary.

There are those who believe that projection of holographic images may be in the billboard's future and that satellites could be easily used to direct images to an electronic billboard. Whatever the future holds, special effects have been with us for a long time and will likely continue to be adapted to outdoor advertising. Thousands of miles of fiber optics lines are already being used to create dramatic effects on billboards. And dare we mention inflatable objects and creatures?

Controlling the lights on outdoor signs has come a long way, but in the future, the same equipment that will regulate the power going to the display will also indicate when lights burn out, record when copy is changed and monitor its condition, and even take regular traffic counts.

Since the day of the first poster, the method of fixing the paper to the board has remained the same. But a new adhesive that overcomes a number of problems has just been developed. Its formula can be adapted to suit the needs of an individual user, accommodating various environmental conditions, for example.

At various points, there has been the temptation to digress at length on the adaptability of the medium to social, commercial, and architectural changes, particularly as a challenge to latter-day detractors who contend that billboards are approaching obsolescence in this highly technical society. But so long as we remain a visually oriented commercial society moving by car, bus, and train from one location to another in the course of the day, it is unlikely that the billboard will pass from the scene.

A recent survey sponsored by the outdoor advertising industry revealed that 25 percent of Americans read the text of all billboards they see and that 50 percent read most, simply because they are "there." These statistics compare favorably when judged against the effectiveness of other media such as television. They are even more pertinent when one considers the statements of marketing specialists who estimated in 1990 that advertisers spend approximately $2.00 per thousand customers with billboards, in comparison with $29.00 per thousand viewers with television.

That billboards are still very much in the media mainstream is attested to by their use by other media. In 1978, newspapers, magazines, radio, and television bought some $21 million in outdoor advertising. By 1989, this figure had risen to $95 million.

A footnote to a commonly held misconception about the prevalence of the billboard: there are fewer billboards today than in 1965, when the Highway Beautification Act went into effect. Over 710,000 signs came down in the subsequent decades. In 1990, 99,790 signs that do not conform to the Beautification Act remained along federal highways. According to industry estimates, changes in land use and new ordinances are reducing the number of these signs by approximately 4,000 each year. Yet industry revenues have increased, mainly from expanded local and regional advertising. Local banks, hospitals, retail stores—all have contributed to the renewed interest in the billboard. In 1990, revenues for the industry were reported to be nearly $1.5 billion.

The industry has historically been responsive to community concerns, such as the public reaction that brought about the Highway Beautification Act. A more recent example is that in 1990 the association called upon its members to limit the placement of messages about products and services that may not be sold to minors.

Granted, there have been industry "bad guys"—and gross abuses among advertisers. This situation will always exist—as in any industry—despite a solid stream of conscientiousness.

More than 20,000 charitable organizations have used the billboard in the past 100 years and by 1990 billboard companies were annually donating more than $140 million in free space to charitable organizations.

The billboard remains in several senses a clean and ethical medium. To be sure, the alcohol and tobacco advertising troubles increasing numbers of Americans, and some of the Sunset Strip boards have touched on the offensive. Still, the billboard cannot be held accountable for fostering violence or contributing to the increasing general degradation of the English language and a whole range of abuses to which other media seem to be increasingly indifferent. It is simply the medium that has told us things we wanted or needed to know, and in color.

With its leaders' traditional genius for adaptability, the billboard will likely continue to do so. This direct, uncomplicated medium remains healthy despite the pronouncements of its cranky detractors. Age seems only to strengthen it.

BIBLIOGRAPHICAL NOTE

While some general works on American advertising contain material on the billboard, the best sources for the study of the billboard are periodicals generated by the outdoor advertising industry and various art direction associations.

The most extensive collection of these primary materials is in the Outdoor Advertising Association Archives at the Florham-Madison Campus Library, Fairleigh Dickinson University, New Jersey. While this collection spans the 100 years of the association's history, it is by no means exhaustive, so considerable use has also been made of the extensive Foster and Kleiser Archives (now Patrick Media Archives) in Los Angeles.

The most useful published sources in preparing this book were the journals, newsletters, and annuals of the billboard industry and the house organs of individual companies. The most valuable publication from the first forty years of the association's history is its monthly journal, with its name changes: *Billposter and Distributor* (New York, 1897–1910); *The Poster* (Chicago, 1910–30); *Advertising Outdoors* (Chicago, 1930–31). Unlike the other monthly industry journals, the *Outdoor Advertising Association News* (Chicago, 1910–65) contained mainly trade news, but it began to provide articles on aesthetic and historical issues when *The Poster* ceased publishing.

The industry's poster annual, first published as a separate publication under the title *Best Posters of the Year* in 1930 (from 1926 to 1929, it was an autumn edition of *The Poster*), continued until 1972 with several changes of name and sponsorship. Without this annual and its attention to detail in the credits and other editorial matter, it would have been difficult to reconstruct the billboard's visual history from 1930 through the sixties. Unfortunately, this publication was discontinued in 1972.

In 1987, an annual publication of award-winning billboards was initiated by the Institute of Outdoor Advertising in order to record the industry's annual "Obie" (for Obelisk) award. This publication, which has changed its name each year, still presents the best billboards, as selected by a committee of experts.

In 1921, the Art Directors Club of New York began an annual of the best advertising of the year, including posters. It is particularly useful in that its content derives from an aesthetic point of view. First titled *Annual of Advertising Art in the United States*, it has changed names from time to time through the years. It is now called *Art Directors Club Annual*.

International Poster Annual (1949–73) and its continuation, *Graphis Posters* (1974 to the present), are helpful to a degree, for their American sections include posters not necessarily found in either of the above publications.

Other useful periodicals are *Signs of the Times* (1906 to the present), published for the outdoor advertising and signage industries, and *Printers' Ink* (1888 to the present), a trade journal of the printing industry, which has reported on the printed poster from time to time.

Then there are those municipal, state, and federal government publications concerned with industry regulation. Most of these began in the early years of the twentieth century and have continued sporadically to the present.

Fortunately, some industry principals, poster artists, and advertising agency personalities who were active in the 1930s are still with us. Yet these lively primary resources are rapidly declining in number. Complementing the wealth of information these individuals offer is the body of correspondence produced by participants in the industry's development, proceedings of annual outdoor advertising conventions, and taped interviews of some of the pioneers. This last group of material is held in the OAAA archive at Fairleigh Dickinson University, Florham-Madison campus.

INDEX

Page numbers in italics refer to illustrations and captions.

Ackerly, Barry, 186
Adams, Wayman, *30*
Advertising Council, *144, 145, 164, 165, 166, 167*
Advertising Outdoors, 54, 71
Alaska Airlines, 157
Albert, Prince, 133
Alcorn, John, 133
Allentown Graphics, 113
Allner, Walter, 113
American Cereal Company, 16
American Chicle Company, 46; *39, 41*
American Civic Association, 14
American Red Cross, 84, 86
American Tobacco Company, 46
AMOCO, 88; *99*
Amtrak, 154
Ancient Age, 107
Anheuser-Busch, 102; *176, 177*
Annual of Advertising Art (1930), 71
Ansco Camera Company, 46
A&P Gypsies, 50
Armitage, Arnold, 54; *62–63, 75*
Armour, 14
Armstrong, Jack, 186
Arrow, *56, 57*
Art Directors Annual Exhibition, 52, 54, 71, 75
Art Directors Club, 52, 71, 86, 88, 91, 108, 113; *54*
Art Directors' Hall of Fame, 52
Art Directors Medal, 88
Art Institute of Chicago, 28, 30
Art in Posters campaign, 46; *30*
Asanger, Jacob, 54; *64, 75*
Associated Advertising Clubs of the World, 24, 30; *32*
Associated Bill Posters' Association, 12, 14; *12, 13, 14, 15*
Association of National Advertisers, 46
Atlantic-Refining, 107
Austin, Charles, 75
Autocar Company, 79
Avedon, Richard, 107
Avis, 126
Ayer, N. W., *117*

Babbitt, B. T., Company, 108
Bab-O, 108
Baker, Ernest Hamlin, 52
Ballantine Ale and Beer, 75; *74, 75*
Barclay, McClelland, 75; *57*
Barnum, P. T., 10; *10, 11*
Barrett, Ross, 186
Bass, Saul, 91, 99, 108, 113, 133; *100–101, 106*
Batten, Barten, Durstine and Osborn (BBDO), 122
Baum, L. Frank, *12*
Bay Advertising Company, 186

Bayer, Herbert, *117, 118*
Beall, Lester, 79, 88
Beaton, Cecil, 107
Beatrice Creamery Company, *50, 51*
Bell, Jared, 10
Bell, W. Rex, 186
Bellows, George, 28
Bemelmans, Ludwig, 113, 129
Benetton, *173*
Benrimo, Thomas, 52
Bernbacn, William, 122, 126
Bernhard, Lucian, 79, 88
Best Foods, 79
Big Hunk, 154
Billboard, 12
Billboard Nuisance, The, 14
Bill Poster, A Monthly Journal Devoted to Outdoor Advertising, The, 12, 16
Billposter and Distributor, 12, 14
Binder, Carla, 79
Binder, Joseph, 75, 79, 88, 91; *74, 75, 84, 90, 91*
Birds Eye, *117, 120–21*
Bit-O-Honey, 154
Blackstock, Joe, 84
Blashfield, Edward, 52
Bloch Brother's Tobacco Company, 46; *39, 40*
Blue Cheer, 113; *112, 113*
Bobri, Vladimir, 88
Bonwit Teller, 79
Boorstin, Daniel, 122
Bourke-White, Margaret, 71
Boy Scouts of America, 48
Bradbury and Houghteling, 10, 12
Bradley, 79, *80*
Bradley, Will H., 16
Breck, George, 28
Brehm, George, *68, 69*
Brinton, Christian, 75, 79
Brodovitch, Alexey, 75, 79, 91
Brown, Denise Scott, 151
Brown, Hal, Sr., 186
Brubaker, Jon, 52
Bruehl, Anton, 71
Brunswick-Panatrope, 50
Bryan, Al, 12, 14
Budweiser, 102; *176, 177*
Buell, Marjorie Henderson, *108*
Bull Durham, 133
Bulova Watch, *64*
Bunte Brothers, 46
Burger King, 133
Burkhart, Charles, 186
Burma Shave, 187
Burtin, Will, 113
Butter-Nut Coffee, 75
Byerly's, 154; *152–53*

California Cooler, 157
California Egg Commission, *179*
California Fruit Growers' Exchange, 46; *42–43*
California Milk Advisory Board, *179*
Calumet Baking Powder, 46
Camel, 52; *48, 49*
Campbell, Robert C., 12
Campbell-Ewald, 129
Campbell Mithun Agency, 129
Campus Crusade for Christ, 148
Carlu, Jean, 88, 91
Carney, Frank and Dan, 133
Casey, F. DeSales, 28; *30*
Cassandre, A.M., 52, 71, 75, 79

Castelli, Leo, 130
Champion Spark Plug Company, 46
Channell Chemical Company, 46
Channel 6, 113; *114*
Chapman, Charles S., 52
Chapman, J. Q. A., 186
Chennell, George L., 46, 186
Cheret, Jules, 16
Chevrolet, 154
Chiat, Jay, 156
Chiat-Day, *156–57*
Chiat/Day/Mojo, 157
Christy, Howard Chandler, 28, 52
Chwast, Seymour, 108; *183*
Citizens Family Welfare Committee, 71
Citizens Housing Council of New York, 79
Civil Rights Bill of 1957, 126
Clark, Frank and Florence, 57
Clarke, René, 52
Cliquot Club Eskimos, 50
Clorox, *102, 103*
Club Med, *183, 184–85*
Cluett-Peabody, *56, 57*
Coca-Cola, 14, 48, 71, 91, 148; *71, 91, 93*
Coffin, Howard E., 24
Coiner, Charles T., 75; *117*
Colgate, 154; *21, 150*
Collier's, 24; *30*
Columbia Records, 88
Combined Communications, 157
Community Chest, 88
Condon, Richard, 186
Container Corporation of America, *117, 118*
Converse, 79
Cooper, Fred G., 52
Coppertone Suntan Lotion, *122, 123*
Cothran, Shirley, 151; *150*
Coty, 126
Crockwell, Douglass, 88
Cusack, Thomas, 12, 186
Cusack, Thomas, Company, 48

Daugherty, James, 28, 52
Davis, Bette, 113
Day, Guy, 156
Deere, John, *157*
Del Mue, Maurice, 54
Denslow, William W., 12; *12, 13*
Dentyne, *21*
Detroit Police Department, 129
Disney Channel, 157
Donaldson, William H., 12
Donnelley, John & Sons, 157, 186
Dorne, Albert, 91
Doyle Dane Bernbach (DDB), 122, 126, 129; *124–25*
Dreyfuss, Leonard, 186
Dr. Pepper, 148; *71*
DuPont, E. I., 79

Eastern Airlines, 107, 126
Edge of the City, 113
Eggers, George William, 30
Eisenmen, Alvin, 133
Ekman, Stanley, 75
El Al, 122
Eller, Carl, 186
Eller Outdoor, 157
Elliott, Elizabeth Shippen Green, 52
Erla, 50
Esquire, 79

Essolene, 75
Estus, Richard, 186
Ex-Lax, 79
Express Mail, 151, 154

Fairbrother, Edwin, *75*
Falls, Charles Buckles, 28, 52; *30*
Fancher, Louis, 24, 28
Federal Highway Act of 1921, 46
Federal Interstate Highway Act of 1954, 113
Federer, C. A., *42–43*
Federico, Gene, 91
Fink, Denman, 52
Firenze, Ettore, 113
Firestone Tire and Rubber Company, 46
First National Bank of Detroit, 54
Fisher, Harrison, 52
Fisk Rubber Company, 46; *30, 31, 38–39*
Fitz, Grancel, 71
Fitzgerald, Frank A., 12
Fizz-Ade, 113; *115*
Flagg, James Montgomery, 28, 30, 52, 88; *32, 33*
Foote, Cone and Belding, 129; *166, 167*
Forbes Magazine, 108; *183*
Ford Motor Company, 46, 48, 154; *75, 77, 96, 97, 129*
Forest Fire Prevention Campaign, 86
Fortune Magazine, 75
Foster, Walter, 186
Foster and Kleiser, 50, 54, 88, 102, 130, 157; *16, 19, 50, 53, 62–63, 71, 73, 75, 79, 91, 173, 175*
Frankenberg, L. von, *66–67*
Frankfurt, Stephen, 126
Fulton, Kerwin, 106, 186
Fulton, Kerwin H., Medal, 75, 88, 91, 113

Gannett Company, Inc., 157
Gannett Outdoor, 54, 157
"Garden Clubs of the Air," 102
Gatorade, 154; *157, 159*
Gaydos, John A., 88
General Electric, 48; *71, 72*
General Foods Corporation, 71; *117, 120–21*
General Outdoor Advertising Company (GOA), 48, 54
Genthe, Arnold, 52
Geoghegan, Walter, 88
Gibson, Charles Dana, 28, 30, 52; *30*
Girl Scouts, 48
Giusti, George, 91
Glaser, Milton, 108
Good Housekeeping, 52
Goodyear, 46
Goss, Harry, 186
Grant, Gordon, 52
Grape Nuts, *134, 137*
Grasset, Eugene, 16
Gray, Bernard, 107
Gray, Fred, *64, 65*
Green, Ben, *122, 123*
Green, Herman, 186
Green, John, *16, 17*
Greene, Milton, *108, 109*
Grimes, David, 50
Gude, O.J., 12, 102, 186; *58, 59*
Gunning, R. J., 186

Hahn, Karl, 122
Hahne Department Store, 102
Hamilton, Richard, 130
Hamshaw, Leonard B., 54

Hardie, Frank, 186
Harper's Bazaar, 75
Harrison, Wallace, 54
Hart, Schaffner & Marx, 46
Hayden, Hayden, 75, 88; *84, 85*
Headlight Overalls, *54, 55*
Heinz, 91
Help Unsell the War, 28
Hendee, George, *22, 23*
Highway Beautification Act of 1965, 113, 188
Hoban, Tana, 107
Hoe, Richard, 10
Hohlwein, Ludwig, 52
Holsum Bread, *134*
Honda, 151, 154, 156; *173, 175*
Hoover, Herbert, *102, 104*
Horn, Steve, 28
Houghteling, C. S., 186
Houston, Herbert S., 24
Howard, John, *117*

Independent, 113
Institute of Outdoor Advertising (IOA), 151; *150*
International Art Service of New York City, 24, *26–27*
International Bill Posters' Association of North America, 10, 12, 14
International Poster Annual, The, 113
International Poster Show, *141, 142–43*
Iodent, 71
Ivory Soap, *60–61*
Izenour, Steven, 151

Jackson, Martha, 130
Jacoby, W. L., *64, 65*
Jantzen, 91; *79, 81*
Jarrett, Charles D., 86
Jax Beer, 107
Jemima, Aunt, 129
Jennings, N. A., 24
Jim Beam, *144*
Johnson, Martin, Company, 22
Johnston, Scott, 107
Judson, Sonia, 54
Justin Boot Company, 154; *171*

Kamchatka, *176*
Karsakov, Leonard, 88
Katz, Joseph, 88
Kauffer, E. McKnight, 50, 91
Kawasaki, 151
Kellogg, 50
Kellogg Switchboard and Supply Company, *64, 65*
Kemps, *178, 179*
Ken-L-Ration, *117, 119*
Kent, Atwater, 50
Kern's, *139*
Klein, Calvin, *172, 173*
Kleiser, George, 50, 106, 186; *64*
Kluge, John, 186
Knoxville Utilities, *144, 146*
Koch, Karl, 54; *71, 73*
Kodak, 46
Koenig, Julian, 122
Koenig and Company, 126
Kool-Aid, *117*
Kroc, Ray, 133
Krone, Helmut, 122
Krush, Joseph, 88
Kubin-Nicholson, 113
Kuppenheimer, 14; *44, 45*

Ladies' Home Journal, The, 14
Lahr, Bert, *126, 127*
Lay's, 126; *126, 127*
Lee, Robert E., 186
Leonard, George, 12
Lerner, George, 91
Levi's, 151
Levy's Jewish Rye, 122
Lewis, Carl, 156
Leyendecker, Francis X., 28
Leyendecker, Joseph C., 52, 88; *34, 44, 45, 56, 57*
Liberty Bond, *32*
Liberty Loan, 28, 30; *34, 35*
Lichtenstein, Roy, 130
Lieblein, Muni, 91
Life, 108; *108, 109*
Lifesavers, *116, 117*
Lincoln Motorcar Company, 58
Link, Barney, 24, 68, 186
Lionni, Leo, 91
"Little Lulu," *108*
Locomobile, 64
Loewy, Raymond, 106
Lois, George, 133
Loomis, Andrew, *60–61, 71, 72*
Los Angeles Brewing Company, 79
Louis, Joe, Private, 126; *88*
Louvre, 108
Lucky Stores, 106
Lucky Strike, 107; *66–67*
Ludekens, Fred, 75, 91
Lundborg, Florence, 186

McCandlish Poster Competition, *74, 75*
McCann-Erickson, 122
McCauley, G. R., 28
McDonald, Richard and Maurice, 130, 133
MacDonald, W. J., 113
McDonald's, 154; *157, 158*
McFarland, J. H., 14
McLaughlin, Jim, 186
McManus, Blanche, 186
McManus, George, 28
McMein, Neysa Moran, 186; *36, 37*
Mail Pouch, 133
Maker's Mark Liquor, *176*
Marlboro, 133; *180–81*
Mars Candy, *133*
Marshall Field, 106
Massachusetts Institute of Technology, 154
Matheuser, Lumir, *75*
Matter, Herbert, 79, 107
Maurer, Sascha, 75, 79
Max, Peter, 133; *144*
Maxwell Company, 186
Mayer, C. Maurice, 54
Meadow Gold, *50, 51*
Melrose, *173*
Metromedia, 130
Metromedia Technologies and Computer Image Systems, 157
Metropolitan Life, *182, 183*
MGM, 113
Milk Foundation of the Twin Cities, 129
Miller, Chester, 84
Minneapolis Institute of Arts, 154; *156*
Minnesota Zoo, *167*
M&Ms, 154
Modess, 107
Moller, Hans, 91
Molyneux, Edward F., 88; *91, 92*

Moon Motor Car Company, 58
Morgan, Wallace, *30*
Morongo Company, 129
Morris Communications, 157
Morton Salt, 107; *130, 131*
Moscoso, Victor, 133
Mothers Against Drunk Driving (MADD), *164*
Munsingwear, 22
Myhre, Eric, 186

Nabisco, *20, 21*
Naegele, R. O., 154, 157, 186
Nason, Ben, 88
National Association of Manufacturers, 84
National Biscuit Company, 14, 48
National Guard, *30*
National Outdoor Advertising Bureau, 16, 68
National Outdoor Advertising Convention, 46; *141, 142–43*
National War Fund, 88
Naugahyde, 126
Newark Billposting Company, 102
New Haven Railroad, 88
"New Media-New Form," 130
New Poster International Exhibition, 75; *78, 79*
New York Billposting Company, 14
New York School of Fine and Applied Art, 30
New York Subways Advertising Company, 91
Nielsen, A. C., 130
Nike, 154, 156; *167, 168–69, 170, 171*
Nissan, 157
Nitsche, Erik, 88
Nixon, Richard, *140, 141*
Norton, Tom, 186
Noxon, Herbert R., 88, 91
Nynex, 157
Nynex Yellow Pages, *161*

OAAA News, 86, 91
Obie, *148, 149, 176*
Office of Civilian Defense, 84, 86
Office of the Coordinator of Inter-American Affairs, 88
Office for Emergency Management, 88
Office of War Information, 91
Ohrbach's, 122
Olivetti, 79
O'Mealia, James F., 14, 186
O'Mealia, Harry, 54, 186
O'Mealia Outdoor Advertising, 54; *141*
100 Best Posters, 71, 79, 86, 107; *64, 65, 68, 75, 76, 94–95*
O'Neill, John, 52
Orr, Garrett P., 91, 96; *98, 99*
Outdoor Advertising Association, 54, 96, 106; *70, 71, 72, 83, 171*
Outdoor Advertising Company, 46
Outdoor Advertising, Inc., 68
Outdoor Advertising—The Modern Marketing Force, 64

Pabco Paint, 99, 113; *100–101*
Pabst, 107; *82–83*
Pacific Telephone, *132, 133*
Paepcke, Walter, *117*
Painted Outdoor Advertising Association, 54
Palmolive Company, 48, 52; *28, 29*
Pan Am, *134, 136*
Papert, 126
Parrish, Maxfield, 16, 46; *30, 31*

Patrick Media Group, 157
Paulson, Carl, 86
Paus, Herbert, 28, 52
Paver, John, 186
Penfield, Edward, 16, 28, 52
Penn, Irving, 107
Pennsylvania State Police, 79
Pepsi-Cola, 148; *102, 105*
Petty, George, 79, 81
Philadelphia Gas Works, 79
Philco, 79
Philley, Clarence U., 186
Phillips-Ramsey agency, *154, 155*
Pillsbury, *12, 13*
Pizza Hut, 133
PM, 75
Pogany, Willy, 28
Polaroid, 122
Porsche, 157
Poster, The, 24, 44, 50, 54, 186
Poster Advertising Association, 24, 28, 46, 48, 54
Pratt, Samuel, 186
Preissig, Voitech, 52
Preminger, Otto, 108; *106*
Procter & Gamble, 113; *60–61, 112, 113*
Push Pin Graphic, The, 108
Push Pin Studios, 108; *130, 131*

Quaker Oats, *16*

Rand, Paul, 91, 108, 133
Rauch, George, 151
RCA, 50, 79
Reebok, 157
Reed, Ethel, 16, 186
Reid, G., *64, 65*
Reid, Marshall, 86; *75, 76*
Reilly, Kevin, Sr., 186
Reuterdahl, Henry, 28; *24, 25*
"Revolutionary Eggs," *130, 131*
Reynolds, Don, 186
Reynolds, R. J., *48, 49*
Rhead, Louis, 16
Riney, Hal, 154
Robbins, Burr W., 186
Rockwell, Norman, 52, 88; *99*
Rocky Road, 154
Roddey, James, 186
Roosevelt, Franklin, 86; *148, 149*
Roosevelt, Theodore, 16, 18
Rosenquist, James, 130
Ruddy, E. L., 186
Ryan, Tom, 79

Safeway Stores, 113
Sahara Hotel, *99*
Sanders, Colonel, 133
San Diego Zoo, 154; *154, 155*
Sanka, *134, 135*
Santa Fe Railway, 129
Sarg, Tony, 186
Sarra, Valentino, 71, 107; *91, 92*
Savignac, Raymond, 108, 113; *112, 113*
Schawinsky, Xanti, 79; *78, 79*
Schmidt, Harold von, 88, 91
Schultz, *126*
Schweppes, 107
Scott, Harold, 52
Scott, Howard, 75, 91; *75, 77, 94–95*
Sealtest, 107
Sears Coldspot refrigerators, 106

Second War Loan drive, 86
Seuss, Dr., 108
7-Up, 148, 151; *144, 147*
Shahn, Ben, 91
Shellane Gas, 75
Shell Gasoline, 71
Shell Motor Oil, 71
Shepard, Dorothy, *82–83*
Shepard, Otis, 75, 79, 91, 108; *70, 71*
Sheridan, Frank, *30*
Sheridan, Jack, 52
"Signs of Life: Symbols in the American City," 151
Silver Flash Gasoline, 75
Simoniz, 107
Skelton, Red, 99
"Smart Women" campaign, *128, 129*
Smith, Dorothy Hope, 52
Smith, Jessie Wilcox, 52
Society of Illustrators, 28, 30; *30*
Sorel, Edward, 108
Southern Pacific Company, 91
Spanish-American War, *14, 15*
Splitdorf, 50
Spreter, Roy, 108; *108, 111*
Stachle, Albert, 75
Stahlbrodt, Edward A., 12
Standard Oil Company, 46
Standard Oil of New Jersey, 86
Steichen, Edward, 71
Steig, William, 79
Steinweiss, Alex, 88
Stevens, William, 54
Stoops, Herbert Morton, 91
Storm Center, 113
Strobridge & Company, *10, 11*
Stroh's, 129
Sucrets, 88
Sundblom, Haddon, 52, 91; *91, 93*
Sunkist, *42–43, 71*
Sun Oil, 79
Sutnar, Ladislav, 108
Suzuki, 151
Swanson, *138, 139*
Syverson, Henry, *132, 133*

Teague, Walter Dorwin, *64*
Teteak, Al, 75
Third War Loan campaign, 86
Thompson, J. Walter, 113, 122; *107*
Thompson, Kenneth W., 91
Thomson-Symon, 113
3M, 96
Tocker, Philip, 186
Toulouse-Lautrec, Henri de, 16
Towne, Charles, 91
Townsend, Harry, *30*
Traffic Audit Bureau, 68
Treidler, Adolph, 28, 52, 88; *30*
Treyser, George A., 186
Trim panel, 157
Turner, Ted, 186
Type Directors Club, 133

Underwood, Clarence, 52; *28, 29*
Uneeda Biscuit, *20, 21*
United Graphics, 113
United Negro College Fund, 154
United Outdoor, 54
U.S. Army, 30
U.S. Army Air Service, 24
U.S. Defense Bonds, 96

U.S. Department of Agriculture, 86, 91; *85, 86*
U.S. Department of Labor, *144, 145*
U.S. Forest Service, *166, 167*
U.S. Navy, 28, 91; *24, 25*
U.S. Office of Facts and Figures, 126
U.S. Post Office Division of Money Orders, 48
U.S. Tire, 58, 59
U.S. Treasury Department, 86; *98, 99*
United Way, 154
Universal Moving Picture Company, 24, *26–27*
Universal Studios, *160, 161*
Utah Oil Refining, 79

Van Beuren, A., Company, 14
Van Beuren, Alfred, 186
Vandsco, 113
Varney and Green, 102
Vehue, Ray, 186
Venturi, Robert, 151
Vickery, John, 79, 86, 108
Vietnam War, *141*
Vincent Printing Company, 113
Vista, 107
Volkswagen, 122, 126, 156; *124–25, 173, 174*
Von Frankenburg, A., 52

WABC radio, 88
Wake Up America Day, 28
Walker, John D., 186
Walker's Deluxe, 129
Wanamaker, John, 79
Warde, Walter T., *91*
War Effort Mobilization campaign, *84, 85, 88, 89*
War Fund campaign, 84
War Manpower campaign, 86
War Production Board, 126
Waterman, L. E., Company, 44; *46, 47*
Watts, Harry, 91, 92
Webber, M. G., Miss, 46
Welch, Jack, 108; *120–21*
Wendy's, 133
Wesson, 52
West Virginia Pulp and Paper, *64*
Whitcomb, Jon, 91
White, Dean, 186
Whitehead, Walter, 52; *54, 55*
Wicks, Ren, 85, 86
Wilbur, Lawrence, 84
Wilkinson, J. W., 96
Williams, John Scott, *34, 35*
Willkie, Wendell, *94–95*
Wilson & Company, 44, 46
Wilson High Ball, 102
Winogrand, Garry, 107
Wonalancet Company, 52
Workman, W. W., 186
World's Fair (New York, 1939), 75
Wright, Jerry, 113
Wrigley, 75, 108, 154; *37, 70, 71*
Wrigley, William, Jr., 48
Wyeth, N. C., 28; *38–39, 71*

Yamaha, 151, 156
Yellow Pages, *132, 133*
Yellowstone Park, 52
Young, Mahonri, 28
Y.M.C.A., *36, 37*
Young and Rubicam, 122, 126
Yucatan Gum, *39, 41*

Zoological Association, 10

CREDITS

The publisher and the OAAA wish to thank the manufacturers, advertising agencies, and archives that permitted the reproduction of images in their possession and supplied the necessary photographs. In all cases, every effort has been made to contact all copyright holders. Should there have been any oversight, we would be happy to update our information.

We are grateful to Lynn Steck for her efforts in gathering the images and assembling the credits below.

Numbers refer to pages on which the illustrations appear. T = top, B = bottom, L = left, R = right.